WAKE UP CALL

WAKE UP CALL

365 Bible readings to start your day

TYNDALE KIDS

Tyndale House Publishers, Inc.
Wheaton, Illinois

Visit Tyndale's exciting Web site at www.tyndale.com

Library of Congress Cataloging-in-Publication Data

Bible. English. New Living Translation. Selections. 2003.
   Wake up call : 365 daily Bible readings to start your day / [compiled by Edythe Draper].
   p. cm.
ISBN 0-8423-7670-4 (alk. paper)
1. Devotional calendars.   I. Draper, Edythe. II. Title.
BS390 .D735 2003
220.5′20834—dc21   2002015186

Printed in the United States of America

07   06   05   04   03
6   5   4   3   2   1

introduction

This book is different in more ways than one. First, it is not a book for you to sit down and read until you are tired of reading. Instead, it is a book for you to read every day, one page at a time. Second, it is not a book written by a person. It is a book written by God, so it should be read carefully. Ask God to speak to you as you read, telling you how he wants you to think and to live in these important days.

God's Word can give us a wake-up call— and help us live the way he wants us to.

JANUARY

No eye has seen, no ear has heard, and no mind has imagined what God has prepared for those who love him.

The eyes of the Lord search the whole earth in order to strengthen those whose hearts are fully committed to him.

Don't let anyone think less of you because you are young. Be an example to all believers in what you teach, in the way you live, in your love, your faith, and your purity.

Take delight in the Lord, and he will give you your heart's desires.

1 Corinthians 2:9; 2 Chronicles 16:9;
1 Timothy 4:12; Psalm 37:4

JANUARY 2

The Son reflects God's own glory, and everything about him represents God exactly. He sustains the universe by the mighty power of his command. After he died to cleanse us from the stain of sin, he sat down in the place of honor at the right hand of the majestic God of heaven.

This shows that God's Son is far greater than the angels, just as the name God gave him is far greater than their names.

Now he is far above any ruler or authority or power or leader or anything else in this world or in the world to come.

Hebrews 1:3-4; Ephesians 1:21

"I am the Alpha and the Omega—the beginning and the end," says the Lord God. "I am the one who is, who always was, and who is still to come, the Almighty One."

Who has done such mighty deeds, directing the affairs of the human race as each new generation marches by? It is I, the Lord, the First and the Last. I alone am he.

God, who began the good work within you, will continue his work until it is finally finished on that day when Christ Jesus comes back again.

Revelation 1:8; Isaiah 41:4; Philippians 1:6

3

JANUARY

4

Let the Lord Jesus Christ take control of you, and don't think of ways to indulge your evil desires.

We are made right in God's sight when we trust in Jesus Christ to take away our sins. And we all can be saved in this same way, no matter who we are or what we have done.

For though your hearts were once full of darkness, now you are full of light from the Lord, and your behavior should show it!

Take no part in the worthless deeds of evil and darkness; instead, rebuke and expose them. When the light shines on them, it becomes clear how evil these things are.

**Romans 13:14; 3:22;
Ephesians 5:8, 11, 13**

5
JANUARY

Live a life filled with love for others, following the example of Christ, who loved you and gave himself as a sacrifice to take away your sins. And God was pleased, because that sacrifice was like sweet perfume to him.

Obscene stories, foolish talk, and coarse jokes—these are not for you. Instead, let there be thankfulness to God.

You can be sure that no immoral, impure, or greedy person will inherit the Kingdom of Christ and of God. For a greedy person is really an idolater who worships the things of this world.

Ephesians 5:2, 4-5

Let your roots grow down into him and draw up nourishment from him, so you will grow in faith, strong and vigorous in the truth you were taught. **Let your lives overflow with thanksgiving for all he has done.**

Don't let anyone lead you astray with empty philosophy and high-sounding nonsense that come from human thinking and from the evil powers of this world, and not from Christ.

The most important piece of clothing you must wear is love.

Colossians 2:7-8; 3:14

JANUARY 6

JANUARY
7

Put away all falsehood and "tell your neighbor the truth" because we belong to each other. And "don't sin by letting anger gain control over you." Don't let the sun go down while you are still angry.

If you are a thief, stop stealing. . . . Don't use foul or abusive language. **Let everything you say be good and helpful, so that your words will be an encouragement to those who hear them.**

Be kind to each other, tenderhearted, forgiving one another, just as God through Christ has forgiven you.

Ephesians 4:25-26, 28-29, 32

Love is patient and kind. Love is not jealous or boastful or proud or rude. Love does not demand its own way. Love is not irritable, and it keeps no record of when it has been wronged.

It is never glad about injustice but rejoices whenever the truth wins out. **Love never gives up, never loses faith, is always hopeful, and endures through every circumstance.**

Love will last forever, but prophecy and speaking in unknown languages and special knowledge will all disappear.

So see to it that you really do love each other intensely with all your hearts.

1 Corinthians 13:4-8; 1 Peter 1:22

I [Jesus] am giving you a new commandment: Love each other. Just as I have loved you, you should love each other.

Don't repay evil for evil. Don't retaliate when people say unkind things about you. Instead, pay them back with a blessing. That is what God wants you to do, and he will bless you for it.

Love covers all offenses.

Let us stop just saying we love each other; let us really show it by our actions. It is by our actions that we know we are living in the truth, so we will be confident when we stand before the Lord.

John 13:34; 1 Peter 3:9; Proverbs 10:12; 1 John 3:18-19

10
JANUARY

I cling to your decrees. Lord, don't let me be put to shame! If you will help me, I will run to follow your commands.

Teach me, O Lord, to follow every one of your principles. Give me understanding and I will obey your law; I will put it into practice with all my heart. Make me walk along the path of your commands, for that is where my happiness is found.

Turn my eyes from worthless things, and give me life through your word.

Psalm 119:31-35, 37

Since we have been made right in God's sight by the blood of Christ, he will certainly save us from God's judgment. For since we were restored to friendship with God by the death of his Son while we were still his enemies, we will certainly be delivered from eternal punishment by his life.

So now we can rejoice in our wonderful new relationship with God—all because of what our Lord Jesus Christ has done for us in making us friends of God.

Romans 5:9-11

12

january

Keep [your parents'] words always in your heart. Tie them around your neck. Wherever you walk, their counsel can lead you. When you sleep, they will protect you. When you wake up in the morning, they will advise you.

For these commands and this teaching are a lamp to light the way ahead of you. **The correction of discipline is the way to life.**

Proverbs 6:21-23

The Lord himself will come down from heaven with a commanding shout, with the call of the archangel, and with the trumpet call of God. First, all the Christians who have died will rise from their graves. Then, together with them, we who are still alive and remain on the earth will be caught up in the clouds to meet the Lord in the air and remain with him forever.

While you are waiting for these things to happen, make every effort to live a pure and blameless life. And be at peace with God.

1 Thessalonians 4:16-17; 2 Peter 3:14

14

JANUARY

The earth is the Lord's, and everything in it. The world and all its people belong to him.

He sends the snow like white wool; he scatters frost upon the ground like ashes.

Then, at his command, it all melts. He sends his winds, and the ice thaws.

He covers the heavens with clouds, provides rain for the earth, and makes the green grass grow in mountain pastures.

He sends peace across your nation and satisfies you with plenty of the finest wheat.

Psalm 24:1; 147:16, 18, 8, 14

O Lord my God, how great you are!
. . . You stretch out the starry curtain
of the heavens; you lay out the rafters
of your home in the rain clouds.

**You placed the world on its
foundation so it would never
be moved.**

At the sound of your rebuke, the
water fled; at the sound of your
thunder, it fled away. Mountains
rose and valleys sank to the levels
you decreed.

Here is the ocean, vast and wide,
teeming with life of every kind, both
great and small. See the ships sailing along, and Leviathan, which you
made to play in the sea.

Psalm 104:1-3, 5, 7-8, 25-26

15

JANUARY

You make the springs pour water into ravines, so streams gush down from the mountains. They provide water for all the animals, and the wild donkeys quench their thirst. The birds nest beside the streams and sing among the branches of the trees.

The trees of the Lord are well cared for—the cedars of Lebanon that he planted. There the birds make their nests, and the storks make their homes in the firs. High in the mountains are pastures for the wild goats, and the rocks form a refuge for rock badgers.

Psalm 104:10-12, 16-18

It is the Lord who created the stars, the Pleiades and Orion. It is he who turns darkness into morning and day into night. It is he who draws up water from the oceans and pours it down as rain on the land. The Lord is his name!

Get to know the God of your ancestors. Worship and serve him with your whole heart and with a willing mind. For the Lord sees every heart and understands and knows every plan and thought. If you seek him, you will find him.

Amos 5:8; 1 Chronicles 28:9

Your sins have cut you off from God. Because of your sin, he has turned away and will not listen anymore. For our sins are piled up before God and testify against us.

But if we confess our sins to him, he is faithful and just to forgive us and to cleanse us from every wrong.

Create in me a clean heart, O God. Renew a right spirit within me.

Isaiah 59:2, 12; 1 John 1:9; Psalm 51:10

JANUARY 18

JANUARY
19

In a wealthy home some utensils are made of gold and silver, and some are made of wood and clay. The expensive utensils are used for special occasions, and the cheap ones are for everyday use. **If you keep yourself pure, you will be a utensil God can use for his purpose.**

Pursue faith and love and peace, and enjoy the companionship of those who call on the Lord with pure hearts.

Christ will make your hearts strong, blameless, and holy when you stand before God our Father on that day when our Lord Jesus comes with all those who belong to him.

2 Timothy 2:20-22; 1 Thessalonians 3:13

20 JANUARY

Many people, including some of the Jewish leaders, believed in him. But they wouldn't admit it to anyone.

God has not given us a spirit of fear and timidity, but of power, love, and self-discipline. So you must never be ashamed to tell others about our Lord.

If anyone acknowledges me [Jesus] publicly here on earth, I will openly acknowledge that person before my Father in heaven.

John 12:42; 2 Timothy 1:7-8; Matthew 10:32

Jesus Christ was revealed as God's Son by his baptism in water and by shedding his blood on the cross—not by water only, but by water and blood. And the Spirit also gives us the testimony that this is true. **So we have these three witnesses—the Spirit, the water, and the blood—and all three agree.** Since we believe human testimony, surely we can believe the testimony that comes from God. And God has testified about his Son.

1 John 5:6-9

22

JANUARY

How can we be sure that we belong to him? By obeying his commandments.

If we continue to live in him, we won't sin either. But those who keep on sinning have never known him or understood who he is.

As we live in God, our love grows more perfect. So we will not be afraid on the day of judgment, but we can face him with confidence because we are like Christ here in this world.

1 John 2:3; 3:6; 4:17

Do you think you deserve credit merely for loving those who love you? Even the sinners do that! And if you do good only to those who do good to you, is that so wonderful? Even sinners do that much!

And if you lend money only to those who can repay you, what good is that? Even sinners will lend to their own kind for a full return.

Love your enemies! Do good to them! Lend to them! And don't be concerned that they might not repay. Then your reward from heaven will be very great, and you will truly be acting as children of the Most High.

Luke 6:32-35

23

24
january

Then God said, "Let us make people in our image, to be like ourselves. They will be masters over all life—the fish in the sea, the birds in the sky, and all the livestock, wild animals, and small animals."

You [God] made all the delicate, inner parts of my body and knit me together in my mother's womb. Thank you for making me so wonderfully complex! . . . You saw me before I was born. **Every day of my life was recorded in your book.**

Everything we have has come from you, and we give you only what you have already given us!

**Genesis 1:26; Psalm 139:13-14, 16;
1 Chronicles 29:14**

Telling lies about others is as harmful as hitting them with an ax, wounding them with a sword, or shooting them with a sharp arrow.

If you want a happy life and good days, keep your tongue from speaking evil, and keep your lips from telling lies. Turn away from evil and do good. Work hard at living in peace with others. **The eyes of the Lord watch over those who do right, and his ears are open to their prayers.** But the Lord turns his face against those who do evil.

Proverbs 25:18; 1 Peter 3:10-12

26

Beware of false prophets who come disguised as harmless sheep, but are really wolves that will tear you apart.

You can detect them by the way they act, just as you can identify a tree by its fruit.

Not all people who sound religious are really godly. They may refer to me [Jesus] as "Lord," but they still won't enter the Kingdom of Heaven. The decisive issue is whether they obey my Father in heaven.

Matthew 7:15-16, 21

May God bless you with his special favor and wonderful peace as you come to know Jesus, our God and Lord, better and better.

As we know Jesus better, his divine power gives us everything we need for living a godly life.

Make every effort to apply the benefits of these promises to your life. Then your faith will produce a life of moral excellence. A life of moral excellence leads to knowing God better.

2 Peter 1:2-3, 5

27
JANUARY

28

If we say we have no sin, we are only fooling ourselves and refusing to accept the truth.

The Lord looks down from heaven on the entire human race; he looks to see if there is even one with real understanding, one who seeks for God. But no, all have turned away from God; all have become corrupt.

But to all who believed him and accepted him, he gave the right to become children of God.

1 John 1:8; Psalm 14:2-3; John 1:12

29

JANUARY

Don't worry about anything; instead, pray about everything. Tell God what you need, and thank him for all he has done.

You should behave . . . like God's very own children, adopted into his family—calling him "Father, dear Father."

Since you are his child, everything he has belongs to you.

So let us come boldly to the throne of our gracious God. There we will receive his mercy, and we will find grace to help us when we need it.

Philippians 4:6; Romans 8:15; Galatians 4:7; Hebrews 4:16

The word of God is full of living power. It is sharper than the sharpest knife, cutting deep into our innermost thoughts and desires. It exposes us for what we really are.

Nothing in all creation can hide from him. Everything is naked and exposed before his eyes.

If you do sin, there is someone to plead for you before the Father. He is Jesus Christ, the one who pleases God completely.

Hebrews 4:12-13; 1 John 2:1

JANUARY 30

JANUARY
31

Be sure that everything is done properly and in order.

This should be your ambition: to live a quiet life, minding your own business and working with your hands.

Listen to your father, who gave you life, and don't despise your mother's experience when she is old. **Get the truth and don't ever sell it; also get wisdom, discipline, and discernment.**

Give your parents joy!

1 Corinthians 14:40; 1 Thessalonians 4:11; Proverbs 23:22-23, 25

1 FEBRUARY

The Lord watches over the path of the godly,
but the path of the wicked leads to destruction.

The Lord will show us who belongs to him
and who is holy.

Your Father, who knows all secrets, will
reward you.

**Search me, O God, and know my heart;
test me and know my thoughts.** Point out
anything in me that offends you, and lead me
along the path of everlasting life.

Such love has no fear because perfect love
expels all fear.

**Psalm 1:6; Numbers 16:5; Matthew 6:4;
Psalm 139:23-24; 1 John 4:18**

For you have been born again. Your new life did not come from your earthly parents because the life they gave you will end in death. But this new life will last forever because it comes from the eternal, living word of God.

Those who believe in me [Jesus], even though they die like everyone else, will live again.

Our earthly bodies, which die and decay, will be different when they are resurrected, for they will never die.

1 Peter 1:23; John 11:25; 1 Corinthians 15:42

3
FEBRUARY

See how very much our heavenly Father loves us, for he allows us to be called his children.

Follow God's example in everything you do, because you are his dear children.

Since we are his children, we will share his treasures—for everything God gives to his Son, Christ, is ours, too.

We do this by keeping our eyes on Jesus, on whom our faith depends from start to finish. He was willing to die a shameful death on the cross because of the joy he knew would be his afterward. Now he is seated in the place of highest honor beside God's throne in heaven.

1 John 3:1; Ephesians 5:1; Romans 8:17; Hebrews 12:2

O Lord, you have examined my heart and know everything about me. You know when I sit down or stand up. You know my every thought when far away. **You chart the path ahead of me and tell me where to stop and rest.** Every moment you know where I am.

You spread out our sins before you—our secret sins—and you see them all.

Nothing in all creation can hide from him. Everything is naked and exposed before his eyes. This is the God to whom we must explain all that we have done.

Psalm 139:1-3; 90:8; Hebrews 4:13

FEBRUARY

4

february

5

I will give you a new heart with new and right desires, and I will put a new spirit in you. **I will take out your stony heart of sin and give you a new, obedient heart.**

The Lord is good and does what is right; he shows the proper path to those who go astray. He leads the humble in what is right, teaching them his way. The Lord leads with unfailing love and faithfulness all those who keep his covenant and obey his decrees.

Lead a life worthy of your calling, for you have been called by God. Be humble and gentle. Be patient with each other, making allowance for each other's faults because of your love.

Ezekiel 36:26; Psalm 25:8-10; Ephesians 4:1-2

6

FEBRUARY

There are six things the Lord hates—no, seven things he detests:

haughty eyes,
a lying tongue,
hands that kill the innocent,
a heart that plots evil,
feet that race to do wrong,
a false witness who pours out lies,
a person who sows discord among brothers.

Obey your father's commands, and don't neglect your mother's teaching. **These commands and this teaching are a lamp to light the way ahead of you.** The correction of discipline is the way to life.

Proverbs 6:16-20, 23

7 FEBRUARY

Share each other's troubles and problems, and in this way obey the law of Christ.

Give to those who ask, and don't turn away from those who want to borrow.

When others are happy, be happy with them. If they are sad, share their sorrow.

Don't let anyone think less of you because you are young. Be an example to all believers in what you teach, in the way you live, in your love, your faith, and your purity.

Galatians 6:2; Matthew 5:42; Romans 12:15; 1 Timothy 4:12

When you give a gift to someone in need, don't shout about it as the hypocrites do—blowing trumpets in the synagogues and streets to call attention to their acts of charity! I assure you, they have received all the reward they will ever get.

But when you give to someone, don't tell your left hand what your right hand is doing. Give your gifts in secret, and your Father, who knows all secrets, will reward you.

Matthew 6:2-4

8
FEBRUARY

Honor those who are your leaders in the Lord's work. They work hard among you and warn you against all that is wrong. Think highly of them and give them your wholehearted love because of their work.

Think of all the good that has come from their lives, and trust the Lord as they do.

Pray . . . for kings and all others who are in authority, so that we can live in peace and quietness, in godliness and dignity.

1 Thessalonians 5:12-13; Hebrews 13:7; 1 Timothy 2:2

10 FEBRUARY

"O Sovereign Lord," I said, "I can't speak for you! I'm too young!" "Don't say that," the Lord replied, "for you must go wherever I send you and say whatever I tell you. **And don't be afraid of the people, for I will be with you and take care of you.**"

Go directly to the Father and ask him, and he will grant your request because you use my name. You haven't done this before. Ask, using my name, and you will receive, and you will have abundant joy.

If you believe, you will receive whatever you ask for in prayer.

Jeremiah 1:6-8; John 16:23-24; Matthew 21:22

Jabez . . . prayed to the God of Israel, "Oh, that you would bless me and extend my lands! **Please be with me in all that I do**, and keep me from all trouble and pain!" And God granted him his request.

God appeared to Solomon in a dream and said, "What do you want? Ask, and I will give it to you!" Solomon replied to God, "Give me wisdom and knowledge to rule . . . properly, for who is able to govern this great nation of yours?"

God gave Solomon great wisdom and understanding. . . . His wisdom exceeded that of all the wise men of the East.

1 Chronicles 4:9-10; 2 Chronicles 1:7-8, 10; 1 Kings 4:29-30

FEBRUARY
11

FEBRUARY
12

The Lord grants wisdom! From his mouth come knowledge and understanding. He grants a treasure of good sense to the godly. **He is their shield, protecting those who walk with integrity.** He guards the paths of justice and protects those who are faithful to him. Then you will understand what is right, just, and fair, and you will know how to find the right course of action every time.

He alone is God.

Proverbs 2:6-9; 1 Timothy 1:17

13 FEBRUARY

Don't put your confidence in powerful people;
there is no help for you there. When their
breathing stops, they return to the earth, and
in a moment all their plans come to an end. **But
happy are those who have the God of Israel
as their helper, whose hope is in the Lord
their God.** He is the one who made heaven and
earth, the sea, and everything in them. He is
the one who keeps every promise forever.

I will be your God throughout your lifetime—
until your hair is white with age.

Psalm 146:3-6; Isaiah 46:4

Don't lose sight of good planning and insight. Hang on to them, for they fill you with life and bring you honor and respect.

I will teach you wisdom's ways and lead you in straight paths. If you live a life guided by wisdom, you won't limp or stumble as you run.

Do not do as the wicked do or follow the path of evildoers. Avoid their haunts. Turn away and go somewhere else.

Look straight ahead, and fix your eyes on what lies before you. **Mark out a straight path for your feet; then stick to the path and stay safe.** Don't get sidetracked; keep your feet from following evil.

We do this by keeping our eyes on Jesus, on whom our faith depends from start to finish. As you endure this divine discipline, remember that God is treating you as his own children.

Proverbs 3:21-22; 4:11-12, 14-15, 25-27; Hebrews 12:2, 7

15
FEBRUARY

If God is for us, who can ever be against us?

The Lord is for me, so I will not be afraid. What can mere mortals do to me?

The Lord is my light and my salvation—so why should I be afraid? Though a mighty army surrounds me, my heart will know no fear. Even if they attack me, I remain confident.

God is with us. He is our leader.

The Lord Almighty is here among us; the God of Israel is our fortress.

Romans 8:31; Psalm 118:6; 27:1, 3; 2 Chronicles 13:12; Psalm 46:7

As evening came, Jesus said to his disciples, "Let's cross to the other side of the lake."

But soon a fierce storm arose. High waves began to break into the boat until it was nearly full of water. Jesus was sleeping at the back of the boat with his head on a cushion. Frantically they woke him up, shouting, "Teacher, don't you even care that we are going to drown?" When he woke up, he rebuked the wind and said to the water, "Quiet down!" Suddenly the wind stopped, and there was a great calm.

Don't worry about anything; instead, pray about everything. Tell God what you need, and thank him for all he has done.

I will lie down in peace and sleep, for you alone, O Lord, will keep me safe.

Mark 4:35, 37-39; Philippians 4:6; Psalm 4:8

16

17

february

Your word is a lamp for my feet and a light for my path.

The Lord says, **"I will guide you along the best pathway for your life.** I will advise you and watch over you. Do not be like a senseless horse or mule that needs a bit and bridle to keep it under control."

Show me the path where I should walk, O Lord; point out the right road for me to follow.

The Lord leads with unfailing love and faithfulness all those who keep his covenant and obey his decrees.

Psalm 119:105; 32:8-9; 25:4, 10

Keep your conscience clear. Then if people speak evil against you, they will be ashamed when they see what a good life you live because you belong to Christ.

For God is pleased with you when, for the sake of your conscience, you patiently endure unfair treatment. Of course, you get no credit for being patient if you are beaten for doing wrong. But if you suffer for doing right and are patient beneath the blows, God is pleased with you.

You should be known for the beauty that comes from within, the unfading beauty of a gentle and quiet spirit, which is so precious to God.

1 Peter 3:16; 2:19-20; 3:4

19

FEBRUARY

Daniel soon proved himself more capable than all the other administrators and princes. Because of his great ability, the king made plans to place him over the entire empire. Then the other administrators and princes began searching for some fault in the way Daniel was handling his affairs, but they couldn't find anything to criticize. He was faithful and honest and always responsible.

So Daniel prospered.

Listen to what the Lord is saying. **The Lord has already told you what is good, and this is what he requires: to do what is right, to love mercy, and to walk humbly with your God.**

Do things in such a way that everyone can see you are honorable.

Daniel 6:3-4, 28; Micah 6:1, 8; Romans 12:17

I will teach you wisdom's ways and lead you in straight paths. If you live a life guided by wisdom, you won't limp or stumble as you run.

Follow God's example in everything you do. . . . Live a life filled with love for others, following the example of Christ, who loved you and gave himself as a sacrifice to take away your sins. And God was pleased, because that sacrifice was like sweet perfume to him.

For though your hearts were once full of darkness, now you are full of light from the Lord, and your behavior should show it!

Proverbs 4:11-12; Ephesians 5:1-2, 8

20
FEBRUARY

21

Pray . . . for kings and all others who are in authority, so that we can live in peace and quietness, in godliness and dignity.

This is good and pleases God our Savior, for he wants everyone to be saved and to understand the truth.

For there is only one God and one Mediator who can reconcile God and people. He is the man Christ Jesus. He gave his life to purchase freedom for everyone.

1 Timothy 2:2-6

22

FEBRUARY

If people persecute you because you are a Christian, don't curse them; pray that God will bless them. When others are happy, be happy with them. If they are sad, share their sorrow. Live in harmony with each other. **Don't try to act important, but enjoy the company of ordinary people.** And don't think you know it all!

Never pay back evil for evil to anyone. Do things in such a way that everyone can see you are honorable. Do your part to live in peace with everyone, as much as possible.

Romans 12:14-18

Remember that the temptations that come into your life are no different from what others experience. And God is faithful. He will keep the temptation from becoming so strong that you can't stand up against it. **When you are tempted, he will show you a way out so that you will not give in to it.**

If God is for us, who can ever be against us?

The Lord is for me, so I will not be afraid. What can mere mortals do to me?

1 Corinthians 10:13; Romans 8:31; Psalm 118:6

FEBRUARY 23

FEBRUARY
24

Just as the mountains surround and protect Jerusalem, so the Lord surrounds and protects his people, both now and forever.

The sun will not hurt you by day, nor the moon at night. The Lord keeps you from all evil and preserves your life. **The Lord keeps watch over you as you come and go, both now and forever.**

I lift my eyes to you, O God, enthroned in heaven. We look to the Lord our God for his mercy, just as servants keep their eyes on their master, as a slave girl watches her mistress for the slightest signal.

My eyes are always looking to the Lord for help, for he alone can rescue me.

Our help is from the Lord, who made the heavens and the earth.

Psalm 125:2; 121:6-8; 123:1-2; 25:15; 124:8

25 FEBRUARY

I pray that you will begin to understand the incredible greatness of his power for us who believe him. This is the same mighty power that raised Christ from the dead and seated him in the place of honor at God's right hand in the heavenly realms. Now he is far above any ruler or authority or power or leader or anything else in this world or in the world to come. **And God has put all things under the authority of Christ**, and he gave him this authority for the benefit of the church. And the church is his body; it is filled by Christ, who fills everything everywhere with his presence.

Ephesians 1:19-23

It was by faith that Abraham offered Isaac as a sacrifice when God was testing him. Abraham, who had received God's promises, was ready to sacrifice his only son, Isaac, though God had promised him, "Isaac is the son through whom your descendants will be counted." Abraham assumed that if Isaac died, God was able to bring him back to life again.

He was absolutely convinced that God was able to do anything he promised.

Is anything too hard for the Lord?

Hebrews 11:17-19; Romans 4:21; Genesis 18:14

27

FEBRUARY

It was by faith that Abel brought a more acceptable offering to God than Cain did. God accepted Abel's offering to show that he was a righteous man. And although Abel is long dead, he still speaks to us because of his faith.

It was by faith that Noah built an ark to save his family from the flood. He obeyed God, who warned him about something that had never happened before. By his faith he condemned the rest of the world and was made right in God's sight.

All these faithful ones . . . were looking for a better place, a heavenly homeland. That is why God is not ashamed to be called their God, for he has prepared a heavenly city for them.

Hebrews 11:4, 7, 13, 16

What is faith? It is the confident assurance that what we hope for is going to happen. It is the evidence of things we cannot yet see.

By faith we understand that the entire universe was formed at God's command, that what we now see did not come from anything that can be seen.

It is impossible to please God without faith. Anyone who wants to come to him must believe that there is a God and that he rewards those who sincerely seek him.

Hebrews 11:1, 3, 6

28

29

february

Humble yourselves before God. Resist the Devil, and he will flee from you. **Draw close to God, and God will draw close to you.** Wash your hands, you sinners; purify your hearts, you hypocrites.

Let there be tears for the wrong things you have done. Let there be sorrow and deep grief. Let there be sadness instead of laughter, and gloom instead of joy. When you bow down before the Lord and admit your dependence on him, he will lift you up and give you honor.

James 4:7-10

As the Scriptures say,

"No one is good—not even one.

No one has real understanding; no one is seeking God.

All have turned away from God; all have gone wrong."

For no one can ever be made right in God's sight by doing what his law commands. **For the more we know God's law, the clearer it becomes that we aren't obeying it.**

Yet now God in his gracious kindness declares us not guilty. He has done this through Christ Jesus, who has freed us by taking away our sins.

Romans 3:10-12, 20, 24

2
MARCH

This Good News was promised long ago
by God through his prophets in the holy
Scriptures. It is the Good News about his
Son, Jesus, who came as a man, born into
King David's royal family line. **And Jesus
Christ our Lord was shown to be the Son
of God when God powerfully raised him
from the dead by means of the Holy Spirit.**
Through Christ, God has given us the
privilege and authority to tell Gentiles
everywhere what God has done for them,
so that they will believe and obey him,
bringing glory to his name.

This Good News tells us how God makes
us right in his sight. This is accomplished
from start to finish by faith. As the Scriptures
say, "It is through faith that a righteous
person has life."

Romans 1:2-5, 17

Everyone who believes that Jesus is the Christ is a child of God. And everyone who loves the Father loves his children, too. We know we love God's children if we love God and obey his commandments. Loving God means keeping his commandments, and really, that isn't difficult. **For every child of God defeats this evil world by trusting Christ to give the victory.** And the ones who win this battle against the world are the ones who believe that Jesus is the Son of God.

1 John 5:1-5

3

MARCH

4

We have a great High Priest who has gone to heaven, Jesus the Son of God. Let us cling to him and never stop trusting him. **This High Priest of ours understands our weaknesses, for he faced all of the same temptations we do, yet he did not sin.** So let us come boldly to the throne of our gracious God. There we will receive his mercy, and we will find grace to help us when we need it.

For the Lord is good. His unfailing love continues forever, and his faithfulness continues to each generation.

Hebrews 4:14-16; Psalm 100:5

5 MARCH

You know how full of love and kindness our Lord Jesus Christ was. Though he was very rich, yet for your sakes he became poor, so that by his poverty he could make you rich.

Since God loved us that much, we surely ought to love each other.

Be kind to each other, tenderhearted, forgiving one another, just as God through Christ has forgiven you.

You must make allowance for each other's faults and forgive the person who offends you. Remember, the Lord forgave you, so you must forgive others.

2 Corinthians 8:9; 1 John 4:11; Ephesians 4:32; Colossians 3:13

In everything you do, stay away from complaining and arguing, so that no one can speak a word of blame against you. You are to live clean, innocent lives as children of God in a dark world full of crooked and perverse people. **Let your lives shine brightly before them.**

Keep your conscience clear. Then if people speak evil against you, they will be ashamed when they see what a good life you live because you belong to Christ.

Philippians 2:14-15; 1 Peter 3:16

MARCH 6

MARCH
7

The Jewish leaders were infuriated by Stephen's accusation, and they shook their fists in rage. **But Stephen, full of the Holy Spirit, gazed steadily upward into heaven and saw the glory of God, and he saw Jesus standing in the place of honor at God's right hand.**

Then they put their hands over their ears, and drowning out his voice with their shouts, they rushed at him. They dragged him out of the city and began to stone him. The official witnesses took off their coats and laid them at the feet of a young man named Saul.

And as they stoned him, Stephen prayed, "Lord Jesus, receive my spirit." And he fell to his knees, shouting, "Lord, don't charge them with this sin!" And with that, he died.

Acts 7:54-55, 57-60

8 MARCH

Be humble and gentle. Be patient with each other, making allowance for each other's faults because of your love.

Be kind to each other, tenderhearted, forgiving one another, just as God through Christ has forgiven you.

You have clothed yourselves with a brand-new nature that is continually being renewed as you learn more and more about Christ, who created this new nature within you.

You, too, must be patient. And take courage, for the coming of the Lord is near.

Ephesians 4:2, 32; Colossians 3:10; James 5:8

[Isaac] reopened the wells his father had dug. . . . His shepherds also dug in the Gerar Valley and found a gushing spring.

But then the local shepherds came and claimed the spring. "This is our water," they said, and they argued over it with Isaac's herdsmen. So Isaac named the well "Argument," because they had argued about it with him. Isaac's men then dug another well, but again there was a fight over it. So Isaac named it "Opposition." Abandoning that one, he dug another well, and the local people finally left him alone.

So don't get tired of doing what is good. Don't get discouraged and give up, for we will reap a harvest of blessing at the appropriate time.

Never pay back evil for evil to anyone.

Genesis 26:18-22; Galatians 6:9; Romans 12:17

10
MARCH

The day of the Lord will come as unexpectedly as a thief. Then the heavens will pass away with a terrible noise, and everything in them will disappear in fire, and the earth and everything on it will be exposed to judgment.

However, no one knows the day or hour when these things will happen, not even the angels in heaven or the Son himself. Only the Father knows. And since you don't know when they will happen, stay alert and keep watch.

The Lord isn't really being slow about his promise to return, as some people think. No, he is being patient for your sake. He does not want anyone to perish, so he is giving more time for everyone to repent.

2 Peter 3:10; Mark 13:32-33; 2 Peter 3:9

As the Scriptures say, "No one is good—not even one.

No one has real understanding; no one is seeking God.

All have turned away from God; all have gone wrong.

No one does good, not even one."

We are made right in God's sight when we trust in Jesus Christ to take away our sins. And we all can be saved in this same way, no matter who we are or what we have done.

Romans 3:10-12, 22

11

12 march

What is impossible from a human perspective is possible with God.

He has the power to do as he pleases among the angels of heaven and with those who live on earth. No one can stop him or challenge him, saying, "What do you mean by doing these things?"

From eternity to eternity I am God. No one can oppose what I do.

Abba, Father . . . everything is possible for you.

I know that you can do anything.

Luke 18:27; Daniel 4:35; Isaiah 43:13; Mark 14:36; Job 42:2

The Lord is merciful and gracious; he is slow to get angry and full of unfailing love. He will not constantly accuse us, nor remain angry forever. He has not punished us for all our sins, nor does he deal with us as we deserve. **For his unfailing love toward those who fear him is as great as the height of the heavens above the earth.** He has removed our rebellious acts as far away from us as the east is from the west. The Lord is like a father to his children, tender and compassionate to those who fear him.

Psalm 103:8-13

14
MARCH

I alone am God. There is no other God; there never has been and never will be. I am the Lord, and there is no other Savior.

I called you by name when you did not know me.

Do you question what I do? Do you give me orders about the work of my hands? I am the one who made the earth and created people to live on it. **With my hands I stretched out the heavens.** All the millions of stars are at my command.

Let all the world look to me for salvation! For I am God; there is no other. . . . Every knee will bow to me, and every tongue will confess allegiance to my name.

Isaiah 43:10-11; 45:4, 11-12, 22-23

The voice of the Lord echoes above the sea. The God of glory thunders. . . . The voice of the Lord is powerful; the voice of the Lord is full of majesty.

The Lord merely spoke, and the heavens were created. . . . He gave the sea its boundaries and locked the oceans in vast reservoirs. For when he spoke, the world began! It appeared at his command.

Who but God goes up to heaven and comes back down? Who holds the wind in his fists? Who wraps up the oceans in his cloak? Who has created the whole wide world? What is his name?

Psalm 29:3-4; 33:6-7, 9; Proverbs 30:4

15
MARCH

16

Now the earth had become corrupt in God's sight, and it was filled with violence. God observed all this corruption in the world, and he saw violence and depravity everywhere.

So God said to Noah, "Look! I am about to cover the earth with a flood that will destroy every living thing. Everything on earth will die! But I solemnly swear to keep you safe in the boat, with your wife and your sons and their wives."

The curse of the Lord is on the house of the wicked, but his blessing is on the home of the upright.

Genesis 6:11-13, 17-18; Proverbs 3:33

17
MARCH

Destruction is certain for those who try to hide their plans from the Lord, who try to keep him in the dark concerning what they do! "The Lord can't see us," you say to yourselves. "He doesn't know what is going on!"

How stupid can you be? **He is the Potter, and he is certainly greater than you.** You are only the jars he makes! Should the thing that was created say to the one who made it, "He didn't make us"? Does a jar ever say, "The potter who made me is stupid"?

Isaiah 29:15-16

It is better to say nothing than to promise something that you don't follow through on.

Dreaming all the time instead of working is foolishness. And there is ruin in a flood of empty words. Fear God instead.

So when you make a promise to God, don't delay in following through, for God takes no pleasure in fools. Keep all the promises you make to him.

And I tell you this, that you must give an account on judgment day of every idle word you speak.

Ecclesiastes 5:5, 7, 4; Matthew 12:36

MARCH 18

MARCH
19

Don't be a fool who doesn't realize that mindless offerings to God are evil. And don't make rash promises to God, for he is in heaven, and you are only here on earth. So let your words be few.

My dear brothers and sisters, be quick to listen, slow to speak, and slow to get angry.

Not all people who sound religious are really godly. They may refer to me as "Lord," but they still won't enter the Kingdom of Heaven. The decisive issue is whether they obey my Father in heaven.

Anyone who listens to my teaching and obeys me is wise.

After Jesus finished speaking, the crowds were amazed at his teaching, for he taught as one who had real authority.

Ecclesiastes 5:1-2; James 1:19; Matthew 7:21, 24, 28-29

Create in me a clean heart, O God. Renew a right spirit within me. **Restore to me again the joy of your salvation, and make me willing to obey you.**

How can I know all the sins lurking in my heart? Cleanse me from these hidden faults. Keep me from deliberate sins! Don't let them control me.

May the words of my mouth and the thoughts of my heart be pleasing to you, O Lord, my rock and my redeemer.

Psalm 51:10, 12; 19:12-14

Blessed are you, O Lord; teach me your principles. I have recited aloud all the laws you have given us. I have rejoiced in your decrees as much as in riches. I will study your commandments and reflect on your ways. I will delight in your principles and not forget your word.

Be good to your servant, that I may live and obey your word. **Open my eyes to see the wonderful truths in your law.** I am but a foreigner here on earth; I need the guidance of your commands. Don't hide them from me!

Psalm 119:12-19

MARCH

22

The law of the Lord is perfect, reviving the soul. The decrees of the Lord are trustworthy, making wise the simple. The commandments of the Lord are right, bringing joy to the heart. The commands of the Lord are clear, giving insight to life. Reverence for the Lord is pure, lasting forever.

The laws of the Lord are true; each one is fair. They are more desirable than gold, even the finest gold. They are sweeter than honey, even honey dripping from the comb.

Fix your thoughts on what is true and honorable and right. Think about things that are pure and lovely and admirable. Think about things that are excellent and worthy of praise.

As for God, his way is perfect. All the Lord's promises prove true. He is a shield for all who look to him for protection. For who is God except the Lord? Who but our God is a solid rock?

Psalm 19:7-10; Philippians 4:8; Psalm 18:30-31

The word of God is full of living power. It is sharper than the sharpest knife, cutting deep into our innermost thoughts and desires. It exposes us for what we really are. Nothing in all creation can hide from him. Everything is naked and exposed before his eyes. This is the God to whom we must explain all that we have done.

Today you must listen to his voice. Don't harden your hearts against him.

Hebrews 4:12-13; 3:15

23

The whole law can be summed up in this one command: "Love your neighbor as yourself." But if instead of showing love among yourselves you are always biting and devouring one another, watch out! Beware of destroying one another.

So I advise you to live according to your new life in the Holy Spirit. Then you won't be doing what your sinful nature craves.

The old sinful nature loves to do evil, which is just opposite from what the Holy Spirit wants.

Galatians 5:14-17

MARCH 25

When you follow the desires of your sinful nature, your lives will produce these evil results: sexual immorality, impure thoughts, . . . quarreling, jealousy, outbursts of anger, selfish ambition, divisions, the feeling that everyone is wrong except those in your own little group. . . .

Let me tell you again, as I have before, that anyone living that sort of life will not inherit the Kingdom of God.

Galatians 5:19-21

26
MARCH

So be careful how you live, not as fools but as those who are wise. Make the most of every opportunity for doing good in these evil days.

Be very careful to obey all the commands. . . . **Love the Lord your God, walk in all his ways, obey his commands, be faithful to him, and serve him with all your heart and all your soul.**

Work hard to prove that you really are among those God has called and chosen. Doing this, you will never stumble or fall away. And God will open wide the gates of heaven for you to enter into the eternal Kingdom of our Lord and Savior Jesus Christ.

**Ephesians 5:15-16; Joshua 22:5;
2 Peter 1:10-11**

And the city has no need of sun or moon, for the glory of God illuminates the city, and the Lamb is its light. The nations of the earth will walk in its light, and the rulers of the world will come and bring their glory to it. Its gates never close at the end of day because there is no night.

Nothing evil will be allowed to enter—no one who practices shameful idolatry and dishonesty—but only those whose names are written in the Lamb's Book of Life.

Revelation 21:23-25, 27

27 MARCH

28

Get rid of all the filth and evil in your lives, and humbly accept the message God has planted in your hearts, for it is strong enough to save your souls.

And remember, it is a message to obey, not just to listen to. If you don't obey, you are only fooling yourself. **For if you just listen and don't obey, it is like looking at your face in a mirror but doing nothing to improve your appearance.** You see yourself, walk away, and forget what you look like. But if you keep looking steadily into God's perfect law—the law that sets you free—and if you do what it says and don't forget what you heard, then God will bless you for doing it.

James 1:21-25

29
MARCH

Gideon replied, "I have one request. Each of you can give me an earring out of the treasures you collected from your fallen enemies." (The enemies, being Ishmaelites, all wore gold earrings.)

"Gladly!" they replied. They spread out a cloak, and each one threw in a gold earring he had gathered.

Gideon made a sacred ephod from the gold and put it in Ophrah, his hometown. But soon all the Israelites prostituted themselves by worshiping it, and it became a trap for Gideon and his family.

Beware that in your plenty you do not forget the Lord your God and disobey his commands, regulations, and laws.

Judges 8:23-25, 27; Deuteronomy 8:11

When the Holy Spirit controls our lives, he will produce this kind of fruit in us: love, joy, peace, patience, kindness, goodness, faithfulness, gentleness, and self-control.

He will give you all you need from day to day if you live for him and make the Kingdom of God your primary concern.

Let us not become conceited, or irritate one another, or be jealous of one another.

Galatians 5:22-23; Matthew 6:33; Galatians 5:26

MARCH 30

MARCH
31

We are instructed to turn from godless living and sinful pleasures. We should live in this evil world with self-control, right conduct, and devotion to God.

Don't hide your light under a basket! Instead, put it on a stand and let it shine for all. **In the same way, let your good deeds shine out for all to see, so that everyone will praise your heavenly Father.**

When he comes we will be like him, for we will see him as he really is. And all who believe this will keep themselves pure, just as Christ is pure.

Titus 2:12; Matthew 5:15-16; 1 John 3:2-3

1 APRIL

If you need wisdom—if you want to know what God wants you to do—ask him, and he will gladly tell you. He will not resent your asking. But when you ask him, be sure that you really expect him to answer, for a doubtful mind is as unsettled as a wave of the sea that is driven and tossed by the wind.

Trust in the Lord with all your heart; do not depend on your own understanding. **Seek his will in all you do, and he will direct your paths.**

He is the eternal King, the unseen one who never dies.

Don't be impressed with your own wisdom. Instead, fear the Lord.

James 1:5-6; Proverbs 3:5-6; 1 Timothy 1:17; Proverbs 3:7

Asa deployed his armies for battle. . . .
Then Asa cried out to the Lord his God,
"O Lord, no one but you can help the power-
less against the mighty! Help us, O Lord
our God, for we trust in you alone. It is in
your name that we have come against this
vast horde. . . . Do not let mere men prevail
against you!"

So the Lord defeated the Ethiopians
in the presence of Asa and the army of
Judah, and the enemy fled.

Praise the Lord! For he has heard my
cry for mercy. **The Lord is my strength,
my shield from every danger.** I trust in
him with all my heart. He helps me.

The Lord protects his people.

2 Chronicles 14:10-12; Psalm 28:6-8

3
APRIL

What a wonderful God we have! How great are his riches and wisdom and knowledge! How impossible it is for us to understand his decisions and his methods! For who can know what the Lord is thinking? Who knows enough to be his counselor? And who could ever give him so much that he would have to pay it back? **For everything comes from him; everything exists by his power and is intended for his glory.**

Give your bodies to God. Let them be a living and holy sacrifice—the kind he will accept. When you think of what he has done for you, is this too much to ask?

Romans 11:33-36; 12:1

"Don't worry about a thing," David told Saul. "I'll go fight this Philistine!"

He picked up five smooth stones from a stream and put them in his shepherd's bag. Then, armed only with his shepherd's staff and sling, he started across to fight Goliath.

Goliath walked out toward David with his shield bearer ahead of him, sneering in contempt.

David shouted in reply, **"You come to me with sword, spear, and javelin, but I come to you in the name of the Lord Almighty**—the God of the armies of Israel, whom you have defied. The Lord does not need weapons to rescue his people. It is his battle, not ours."

So David triumphed over the Philistine giant with only a stone and sling.

Our . . . power and success come from God.

1 Samuel 17:32, 40-42, 45, 47, 50; 2 Corinthians 3:5

5
april

We can rejoice, too, when we run into problems and trials, for we know that they are good for us—they help us learn to endure.

We know how dearly God loves us, because he has given us the Holy Spirit to fill our hearts with his love.

As you endure this divine discipline, remember that God is treating you as his own children. Whoever heard of a child who was never disciplined? **If God doesn't discipline you as he does all of his children, it means that you are illegitimate and are not really his children after all.**

No discipline is enjoyable while it is happening—it is painful! But afterward there will be a quiet harvest of right living.

Let your roots grow down into him and draw up nourishment from him, so you will grow in faith, strong and vigorous in the truth.

Romans 5:3, 5; Hebrews 12:7-8, 11; Colossians 2:7

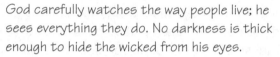

God carefully watches the way people live; he sees everything they do. No darkness is thick enough to hide the wicked from his eyes.

Do not be afraid of the terrors of the night, nor fear the dangers of the day, nor dread the plague that stalks in darkness, nor the disaster that strikes at midday.

The Lord himself watches over you! . . . The sun will not hurt you by day, nor the moon at night. The Lord keeps you from all evil and preserves your life.

Job 34:21-22; Psalm 91:5-6; 121:5-7

7 APRIL

In the last days there will be very difficult times. For people will love only themselves and their money. They will be boastful and proud, scoffing at God, disobedient to their parents, and ungrateful. They will consider nothing sacred. They will be unloving and unforgiving; they will slander others and have no self-control; they will be cruel, and have no interest in what is good. They will betray their friends, be reckless, be puffed up with pride, and love pleasure rather than God. They will act as if they are religious, but they will reject the power that could make them godly. You must stay away from people like that.

You must remain faithful to the things you have been taught.

2 Timothy 3:1-5, 14

One of them, an expert in religious law, tried to trap him with this question: "Teacher, which is the most important commandment in the law of Moses?"

Jesus replied, "'**You must love the Lord your God with all your heart, all your soul, and all your mind.**' This is the first and greatest commandment. A second is equally important: 'Love your neighbor as yourself.' All the other command-ments and all the demands of the prophets are based on these two commandments."

Matthew 22:35-40

8
APRIL

What is causing the quarrels and fights among you? Isn't it the whole army of evil desires at war within you? You want what you don't have, . . . so you fight and quarrel to take it away from [others].

It is foolish to belittle a neighbor; a person with good sense remains silent.

The tongue is a small thing, but what enormous damage it can do.

Don't speak evil against each other, my dear brothers and sisters. If you criticize each other and condemn each other, then you are criticizing and condemning God's law.

Humble yourselves before God. Resist the Devil, and he will flee from you.

James 4:1-2; Proverbs 11:12; James 3:5; 4:11, 7

10
APRIL

Turn from your sins! . . . Put all your rebellion
behind you, and get for yourselves a new heart
and a new spirit.

**Use every piece of God's armor to resist
the enemy in the time of evil, so that after
the battle you will still be standing firm**.

Get rid of all the filth and evil in your lives,
and humbly accept the message God has
planted in your hearts, for it is strong enough
to save your souls.

Ezekiel 18:30-31; Ephesians 6:13; James 1:21

God showed his great love for us by sending Christ to die for us while we were still sinners.

He personally carried away our sins in his own body on the cross so we can be dead to sin and live for what is right.

He was oppressed and treated harshly, yet he never said a word. **He was led as a lamb to the slaughter.** And as a sheep is silent before the shearers, he did not open his mouth. From prison and trial they led him away to his death.

Since Christ suffered physical pain, you must arm yourselves with the same attitude he had, and be ready to suffer, too.

Romans 5:8; 1 Peter 2:24; Isaiah 53:7-8; 1 Peter 4:1

APRIL

Pilate had Jesus flogged with a lead-tipped whip.
The soldiers made a crown of long, sharp thorns
and put it on his head, and they put a royal purple
robe on him. "Hail! King of the Jews!" they mocked,
and they hit him with their fists.

When they saw him, the leading priests and
Temple guards began shouting, "Crucify! Crucify!"

He was wounded and crushed for our sins.
He was beaten that we might have peace. He was
whipped, and we were healed! . . . The Lord laid
on him the guilt and sins of us all.

John 19:1-3, 6; Isaiah 53:5-6

13 APRIL

It was nine o'clock in the morning when the crucifixion took place.

The people passing by shouted abuse, shaking their heads in mockery.

The leading priests and teachers of religious law also mocked Jesus. . . . Even the two criminals who were being crucified with Jesus ridiculed him.

Then . . . Jesus called out with a loud voice, *"Eloi, Eloi, lema sabachthani?"* which means, **"My God, my God, why have you forsaken me?"**

Then Jesus uttered another loud cry and breathed his last.

When the Roman officer who stood facing him saw how he had died, he exclaimed, "Truly, this was the Son of God!"

Mark 15:25, 29, 31-32, 34, 37, 39

As the new day was dawning, Mary Magdalene and the other Mary went out to see the tomb. Suddenly there was a great earthquake, because an angel of the Lord came down from heaven.

The angel spoke to the women. "Don't be afraid!" he said. "I know you are looking for Jesus, who was crucified. **He isn't here! He has been raised from the dead, just as he said would happen**."

Christ died and rose again for this very purpose, so that he might be Lord of those who are alive and of those who have died.

Matthew 28:1-2, 5-6; Romans 14:9

15
APRIL

Show me the path where I should walk, O Lord; point out the right road for me to follow. Lead me by your truth and teach me, for you are the God who saves me. All day long I put my hope in you.

Forgive the rebellious sins of my youth; look instead through the eyes of your unfailing love.

The Lord is good and does what is right; he shows the proper path to those who go astray. He leads the humble in what is right, teaching them his way. The Lord leads with unfailing love and faithfulness all those who keep his covenant and obey his decrees.

Psalm 25:4-5, 7-10

The Lord is for me, so I will not be afraid. What can mere mortals do to me?

My health may fail, and my spirit may grow weak, but God remains the strength of my heart; he is mine forever.

The Lord is good. When trouble comes, he is a strong refuge. And he knows everyone who trusts in him.

How good it is to be near God! I have made the Sovereign Lord my shelter, and I will tell everyone about the wonderful things you do.

Psalm 118:6; 73:26; Nahum 1:7; Psalm 73:28

16

17

april

Who will want to harm you if you are eager to
do good? But even if you suffer for doing what
is right, God will reward you for it. . . . You
must worship Christ as Lord of your life. **And
if you are asked about your Christian hope,
always be ready to explain it.** But you must
do this in a gentle and respectful way.

Keep your conscience clear. Then if people
speak evil against you, they will be ashamed
when they see what a good life you live because
you belong to Christ. Remember, it is better to
suffer for doing good, if that is what God wants,
than to suffer for doing wrong!

Christ also suffered when he died . . . that he
might bring us safely home to God.

1 Peter 3:13-18

APRIL

18

Don't let anyone think less of you because you
are young. Be an example to all believers in what
you teach, in the way you live, in your love, your
faith, and your purity.

It's wonderful to be young! Enjoy every
minute of it. Do everything you want to do; take
it all in. But remember that you must give an
account
to God for everything you do. So banish grief
and pain, but remember that youth, with a
whole life before it, still faces the threat of
meaninglessness.

1 Timothy 4:12; Ecclesiastes 11:9-10

19

APRIL

Caleb tried to encourage the people as they stood before Moses. "Let's go at once to take the land," he said. "We can certainly conquer it!"

But the other men who had explored the land with him answered, "We can't go up against them! They are stronger than we are!"

When I am afraid, I put my trust in you. O God, I praise your word. I trust in God, so why should I be afraid? What can mere mortals do to me?

On the very day I call to you for help, my enemies will retreat. This I know: God is on my side.

Numbers 13:30-31; Psalm 56:3-4, 9

None of us can hold back our spirit from departing. None of us has the power to prevent the day of our death.

We know that when this earthly tent we live in is taken down—when we die and leave these bodies—we will have a home in heaven, an eternal body made for us by God himself and not by human hands.

We are fully confident, and we would rather be away from these bodies, for then we will be at home with the Lord.

**Ecclesiastes 8:8;
2 Corinthians 5:1, 8**

20
APRIL

There are many rooms in my Father's home, and I am going to prepare a place for you. . . . When everything is ready, I will come and get you, so that you will always be with me where I am.

All these faithful ones . . . saw it all from a distance and welcomed the promises of God. **They agreed that they were no more than foreigners and nomads here on earth.** And obviously people who talk like that are looking forward to a country they can call their own.

Together with them, we who are still alive and remain on the earth will be caught up in the clouds to meet the Lord in the air and remain with him forever.

**John 14:2-3; Hebrews 11:13-14;
1 Thessalonians 4:17**

22
APRIL

The Lord doesn't make decisions the way you do! **People judge by outward appearance, but the Lord looks at a person's thoughts and intentions.**

Let the people turn from their wicked deeds. Let them banish from their minds the very thought of doing wrong! Let them turn to the Lord that he may have mercy on them. Yes, turn to our God, for he will abundantly pardon.

The Lord's delight is in those who honor him, those who put their hope in his unfailing love.

1 Samuel 16:7; Isaiah 55:7; Psalm 147:11

Am I a God who is only in one place? . . . Can anyone hide from me? Am I not everywhere in all the heavens and earth?

O Lord . . . you know when I sit down or stand up. You know my every thought when far away. You chart the path ahead of me and tell me where to stop and rest. Every moment you know where I am. You know what I am going to say before I say it.

Nothing in all creation can hide from him. Everything is naked and exposed before his eyes. This is the God to whom we must explain all that we have done.

Jeremiah 23:23-24; Psalm 139:1-4; Hebrews 4:13

APRIL

No amount of soap or lye can make you clean. You are stained with guilt that cannot be washed away.

Yet now God in his gracious kindness declares us not guilty. He has done this through Christ Jesus, who has freed us by taking away our sins. For God sent Jesus to take the punishment for our sins and to satisfy God's anger against us.

Jeremiah 2:22; Romans 3:24-25

25 APRIL

In the beginning the Word already existed.

He created everything there is. Nothing exists that he didn't make.

But although the world was made through him, the world didn't recognize him when he came. Even in his own land and among his own people, he was not accepted. But to all who believed him and accepted him, he gave the right to become children of God.

John 1:1, 3, 10-12

When Jesus arrived in Capernaum, a Roman officer came and pleaded with him, "Lord, my young servant lies in bed, paralyzed and racked with pain."

Jesus said, "I will come and heal him."

Then the officer said, "Lord, I am not worthy to have you come into my home. Just say the word from where you are, and my servant will be healed! I know, because I am under the authority of my superior officers and I have authority over my soldiers. I only need to say, 'Go,' and they go, or 'Come,' and they come. And if I say to my slaves, 'Do this or that,' they do it."

When Jesus heard this, he was amazed. Turning to the crowd, he said, "I tell you the truth, I haven't seen faith like this in all the land of Israel!"

[God] is able to accomplish infinitely more than we would ever dare to ask or hope.

**Matthew 8:5-10;
Ephesians 3:20**

Have you ever commanded the morning to appear and caused the dawn to rise in the east? Have you ever told the daylight to spread to the ends of the earth?

Where does the light come from, and where does the darkness go? Can you take it to its home? Do you know how to get there?

God said, "Let there be light," and there was light. God called the light "day" and the darkness "night." Together these made up one day.

Job 38:12-13, 19-20; Genesis 1:3, 5

O Lord, what a variety of things you have made!

You send the darkness, and it becomes night, when all the forest animals prowl about. Then the young lions roar for their food, but they are dependent on God. At dawn they slink back into their dens to rest. Then people go off to their work; they labor until the evening shadows fall again.

Here is the ocean, vast and wide, teeming with life of every kind, both great and small. See the ships sailing along, and Leviathan, which you made to play in the sea.

In wisdom you have made them all. The earth is full of your creatures.

Psalm 104:24a, 20-23, 25-26, 24b

28

april

29

Moses told the people, "Don't be afraid. Just stand where you are and watch the Lord rescue you."

Moses raised his hand over the sea, and the Lord opened up a path through the water. . . . **So the people of Israel walked through the sea on dry ground, with walls of water on each side!** Then the Egyptians . . . followed them across the bottom of the sea.

When all the Israelites were on the other side . . . the water roared back into its usual place, and the Lord swept the terrified Egyptians into the surging currents.

Praise the Lord, for he has shown me his unfailing love. He kept me safe when my city was under attack.

Exodus 14:13, 21-23, 26-27; Psalm 31:21

APRIL 30

I will not abandon you as orphans—I will come to you.

I am with you always, even to the end of the age.

I am the living one who died. Look, I am alive forever and ever!

That is why we can say with confidence, "The Lord is my helper, so I will not be afraid. What can mere mortals do to me?"

If my father and mother abandon me, the Lord will hold me close.

John 14:18; Matthew 28:20; Revelation 1:18; Hebrews 13:6; Psalm 27:10

1 MAY

From prison and trial they led him away to his death. **But who among the people realized that he was dying for their sins—that he was suffering their punishment?** He had done no wrong, and he never deceived anyone. But he was buried like a criminal; he was put in a rich man's grave.

But it was the Lord's good plan to crush him and fill him with grief. Yet when his life is made an offering for sin, he will have a multitude of children, many heirs. He will enjoy a long life, and the Lord's plan will prosper in his hands.

Isaiah 53:8-10

Since Christ suffered physical pain, you must arm yourselves with the same attitude he had, and be ready to suffer, too. . . . And you won't spend the rest of your life chasing after evil desires, but you will be anxious to do the will of God.

Of course, your former friends are very surprised when you no longer join them in the wicked things they do, and they say evil things about you. But just remember that they will have to face God, who will judge everyone, both the living and the dead.

1 Peter 4:1-2, 4-5

2 MAY

3

For a child is born to us, a son is given to us. And the government will rest on his shoulders. These will be his royal titles:

Wonderful Counselor,
Mighty God,
Everlasting Father,
Prince of Peace.

His ever expanding, peaceful government will never end. **He will rule forever with fairness and justice.**

Isaiah 9:6-7

4 MAY

The Lord isn't really being slow about his promise
to return. . . . he is being patient for your sake.
**He does not want anyone to perish, so he is
giving more time for everyone to repent.**

But we are looking forward to the new heavens
and new earth he has promised, a world where
everyone is right with God.

While you are waiting for these things to
happen, make every effort to live a pure and
blameless life. And be at peace with God.

2 Peter 3:9, 13-14

Live in a manner worthy of the Good News about Christ.

Keep away from every kind of evil.

Be happy if you are insulted for being a Christian.

In everything you do, stay away from complaining and arguing, so that no one can speak a word of blame against you. **You are to live clean, innocent lives as children of God in a dark world full of crooked and perverse people.** Let your lives shine brightly before them.

Never let loyalty and kindness get away from you! Wear them like a necklace; write them deep within your heart.

Philippians 1:27; 1 Thessalonians 5:22; 1 Peter 4:14; Philippians 2:14-15; Proverbs 3:3

MAY

5

MAY
6

I [Jesus] have come as a light to shine in this dark world, so that all who put their trust in me will no longer remain in the darkness.

Though your hearts were once full of darkness, now you are full of light from the Lord, and your behavior should show it! For this light within you produces only what is good and right and true. Try to find out what is pleasing to the Lord.

Love comes from God. Anyone who loves is born of God and knows God. But anyone who does not love does not know God—for God is love.

John 12:46; Ephesians 5:8-10; 1 John 4:7-8

7 MAY

Fear of the Lord is the beginning of knowledge. Only fools despise wisdom and discipline.

Listen, my child, to what your father teaches you. Don't neglect your mother's teaching. What you learn from them will crown you with grace and clothe you with honor.

But you must remain faithful to the things you have been taught. . . . They have given you the wisdom to receive the salvation that comes by trusting in Christ Jesus.

Proverbs 1:7-9; 2 Timothy 3:14-15

You have been taught the holy Scriptures from childhood, and they have given you the wisdom to receive the salvation that comes by trusting in Christ Jesus.

All Scripture is inspired by God and is useful to teach us what is true and to make us realize what is wrong in our lives. It straightens us out and teaches us to do what is right. It is God's way of preparing us in every way, fully equipped for every good thing God wants us to do.

2 Timothy 3:15-17

9
MAY

Examine yourselves to see if your
faith is really genuine. Test yourselves. If you cannot tell that Jesus
Christ is among you, it means you
have failed the test.

If someone says, "I belong to God,"
but doesn't obey God's commandments, that person is a liar and does
not live in the truth. **But those who
obey God's word really do love him.**
That is the way to know whether or
not we live in him. Those who say
they live in God should live their
lives as Christ did.

2 Corinthians 13:5; 1 John 2:4-6

Work hard and cheerfully at whatever you do, as though you were working for the Lord rather than for people. Remember that the Lord will give you an inheritance as your reward, and **the Master you are serving is Christ.**

But if you do what is wrong, you will be paid back for the wrong you have done. For God has no favorites who can get away with evil.

Colossians 3:23-25

11 may

Pride leads to disgrace.

Claiming to be wise, they became utter fools instead.

If you think you are standing strong, be careful, for you, too, may fall into the same sin.

Though you soar as high as eagles and build your nest among the stars, I will bring you crashing down. I, the Lord, have spoken!

**Proverbs 11:2; Romans 1:22;
1 Corinthians 10:12; Obadiah 1:4**

MAY 12

The Lord is high above the nations; his glory is far greater than the heavens. Far below him are the heavens and the earth. He stoops to look, and he lifts the poor from the dirt and the needy from the garbage dump. He sets them among princes.

The unfailing love of the Lord never ends! . . . His mercies begin afresh each day.

Psalm 113:4, 6-8; Lamentations 3:22-23

13 MAY

Salvation that comes from trusting Christ . . . is already within easy reach. In fact, the Scriptures say, "The message is close at hand; it is on your lips and in your heart."

For if you confess with your mouth that Jesus is Lord and believe in your heart that God raised him from the dead, you will be saved. For it is by believing in your heart that you are made right with God, and it is by confessing with your mouth that you are saved.

As the Scriptures tell us, "Anyone who believes in him will not be disappointed."

Romans 10:8-11

For God is working in you, giving you the desire to obey him and the power to do what pleases him.

Don't ignore it when the Lord disciplines you, and don't be discouraged when he corrects you. **For the Lord corrects those he loves, just as a father corrects a child in whom he delights.**

Then everyone will give honor to the name of our Lord Jesus because of you, and you will be honored along with him.

Philippians 2:13; Proverbs 3:11-12; 2 Thessalonians 1:12

14 MAY

15

O Lord, our Lord, the majesty of your name fills the earth! Your glory is higher than the heavens. You have taught children and nursing infants to give you praise. They silence your enemies who were seeking revenge.

I will thank you, Lord, with all my heart; I will tell of all the marvelous things you have done.

Turn us again to yourself, O Lord God Almighty. Make your face shine down upon us. Only then will we be saved.

Psalm 8:1-2; 9:1; 80:19

16 MAY

I turned away from God, but then I was sorry. I kicked myself for my stupidity!

The Lord still waits for you to come to him so he can show you his love. . . . Blessed are those who wait for him to help them.

You will hear a voice say, "This is the way; turn around and walk here."

Our lives are in his hands, and he keeps our feet from stumbling.

Jeremiah 31:19; Isaiah 30:18, 21; Psalm 66:9

Food and drink . . . is from the hand of God. For who can eat or enjoy anything apart from him?

You send rain on the mountains from your heavenly home, and you fill the earth with the fruit of your labor. You cause grass to grow for the cattle. You cause plants to grow for people to use.

He gives food to every living thing. **His faithful love endures forever.** Give thanks to the God of heaven.

Ecclesiastes 2:24-25;
Psalm 104:13-14; 136:25-26

MAY

MAY
18

It is good to give thanks to the Lord. . . . It is good to proclaim your unfailing love in the morning, your faithfulness in the evening.

Come before him with thanksgiving. For the Lord is a great God, the great King above all gods. He owns the depths of the earth, and even the mightiest mountains are his. The sea belongs to him, for he made it. His hands formed the dry land, too.

He is our God. We are the people he watches over, the sheep under his care.

Psalm 92:1-2; 95:2-5, 7

David shouted in reply, "You come to me with sword, spear, and javelin, but I come to you in the name of the Lord Almighty—the God of the armies of Israel, whom you have defied."

Reaching into his shepherd's bag and taking out a stone, [David] hurled it from his sling and hit the Philistine in the forehead. The stone sank in, and Goliath stumbled and fell face downward to the ground. So David triumphed over the Philistine giant with only a stone and sling.

The best-equipped army cannot save a king, nor is great strength enough to save a warrior. **But the Lord watches over those who fear him, those who rely on his unfailing love.**

1 Samuel 17:45, 49-50; Psalm 33:16, 18

Keep on asking, and you will be given what you ask for. Keep on looking, and you will find. Keep on knocking, and the door will be opened. For everyone who asks, receives. Everyone who seeks, finds. And the door is opened to everyone who knocks.

And we can be confident that he will listen to us whenever we ask him for anything in line with his will. And if we know he is listening when we make our requests, we can be sure that he will give us what we ask for.

Matthew 7:7-8; 1 John 5:14-15

21
MAY

What does the Lord your God require of you? He requires you to fear him, to live according to his will, to love and worship him with all your heart and soul, and to obey the Lord's commands and laws that I am giving you today for your own good.

You will keep in perfect peace all who trust in you, whose thoughts are fixed on you! Trust in the Lord always, for the Lord God is the eternal Rock.

For those who are righteous, the path is not steep and rough. You are a God of justice, and you smooth out the road ahead of them.

**Deuteronomy 10:12-13;
Isaiah 26:3-4, 7**

Don't lie to each other, for you have stripped off your old evil nature and all its wicked deeds. In its place you have clothed yourselves with a brand-new nature that is continually being renewed as you learn more and more about Christ, who created this new nature within you. In this new life, it doesn't matter if you are a Jew or a Gentile, circumcised or uncircumcised, barbaric, uncivilized, slave, or free. **Christ is all that matters,** and he lives in all of us.

Colossians 3:9-11

22

The Lord says: "The people . . . have sinned again and again, and I will not forget it.

"I will make you groan as a wagon groans when it is loaded down with grain. Your fastest runners will not get away. The strongest among you will become weak. **Even the mightiest warriors will be unable to save themselves.** The archers will fail to stand their ground. The swiftest soldiers won't be fast enough to escape. Even warriors on horses won't be able to outrun the danger. On that day, the most courageous of your fighting men will drop their weapons and run for their lives. I, the Lord, have spoken!"

God has come in this way to show you his awesome power. From now on, let your fear of him keep you from sinning!

Amos 1:3; 2:13-16; Exodus 20:20

God will judge us for everything we do, including every secret thing, whether good or bad.

Lord, if you kept a record of our sins, who, O Lord, could ever survive? But you offer forgiveness, that we might learn to fear you.

He has not punished us for all our sins, nor does he deal with us as we deserve. For his unfailing love toward those who fear him is as great as the height of the heavens above the earth.

Ecclesiastes 12:14; Psalm 130:3-4; 103:10-11

25 MAY

Their ways are futile and foolish. They cut down a tree and carve an idol. They decorate it with gold and silver and then fasten it securely with hammer and nails so it won't fall over. There stands their god like a helpless scarecrow in a garden! It cannot speak, and it needs to be carried because it cannot walk. Do not be afraid of such gods, for they can neither harm you nor do you any good.

Lord, there is no one like you! For you are great, and your name is full of power.

Jeremiah 10:3-6

Great and marvelous are your actions,
    Lord God Almighty.
Just and true are your ways,
    O King of the nations.
    Who will not fear, O Lord, and
        glorify your name?
    For you alone are holy.

Revelation 15:3-4

26
MAY

Even the heavens cannot be absolutely pure in his sight.

The moon and stars scarcely shine compared to him.

Who else among the gods is like you, O Lord? Who is glorious in holiness like you?

Be holy in everything you do, just as God—who chose you to be his children—is holy.

Make every effort to live a pure and blameless life. And be at peace with God.

Job 15:15; 25:5; Exodus 15:11; 1 Peter 1:15; 2 Peter 3:14

28 MAY

The Lord is a God who knows your deeds; and he will judge you for what you have done.

Don't be misled. Remember that you can't ignore God and get away with it. **You will always reap what you sow!** Those who live only to satisfy their own sinful desires will harvest the consequences of decay and death.

And how do you benefit if you gain the whole world but lose your own soul in the process? Is anything worth more than your soul?

1 Samuel 2:3; Galatians 6:7-8; Matthew 16:26

Don't team up with those who are unbelievers. How can goodness be a partner with wickedness? How can light live with darkness? What harmony can there be between Christ and the Devil? How can a believer be a partner with an unbeliever?

Stop loving this evil world and all that it offers you, for when you love the world, you show that you do not have the love of the Father in you.

Don't copy the behavior and customs of this world, but let God transform you into a new person by changing the way you think.

2 Corinthians 6:14-15; 1 John 2:15; Romans 12:2

Take a lesson from the ants.

They aren't strong, but they store up food for the winter.

Learn from their ways and be wise! Even though they have no prince, governor, or ruler to make them work, they labor hard all summer, gathering food for the winter.

Hard work means prosperity; only fools idle away their time.

Proverbs 6:6a; 30:25; 6:6b-8; 12:11

31 MAY

I want you to share your food with the hungry
and to welcome poor wanderers into your homes.
Give clothes to those who need them, and do not
hide from relatives who need your help.
Feed the hungry and help those in trouble.
Then your light will shine out from the darkness, and the darkness around you will be as
bright as day.

You are the light of the world—like a city
on a mountain, glowing in the night for all
to see . . . so that everyone will praise your
heavenly Father.

Isaiah 58:7, 10; Matthew 5:14, 16

I am not writing a new commandment, for it is an old one you have always had, right from the beginning. **This commandment—to love one another—is the same message you heard before.** Yet it is also new. This commandment is true in Christ and is true among you, because the darkness is disappearing and the true light is already shining.

For though your hearts were once full of darkness, now you are full of light from the Lord, and your behavior should show it!

1 John 2:7-8; Ephesians 5:8

2
JUNE

Love comes from God. Anyone who loves is born of God and knows God. But anyone who does not love does not know God—for God is love.

God showed how much he loved us by sending his only Son into the world so that we might have eternal life through him.

Since God loved us that much, we surely ought to love each other. No one has ever seen God. But if we love each other, God lives in us, and his love has been brought to full expression through us.

1 John 4:7-9, 11-12

God did not spare even his own Son but gave him up for us all.

Everyone who believes in him will . . . have eternal life.

There is salvation in no one else! There is no other name in all of heaven for people to call on to save them.

All glory to God, who is able to keep you from stumbling, and who will bring you into his glorious presence innocent of sin and with great joy.

Romans 8:32; John 3:16b; Acts 4:12; Jude 1:24

4
june

If you are asked about your Christian hope, always be ready to explain it. But you must do this in a gentle and respectful way.

Gently teach those who oppose the truth. Perhaps God will change those people's hearts, and they will believe the truth.

Live wisely among those who are not Christians, and make the most of every opportunity. Let your conversation be gracious and effective so that you will have the right answer for everyone.

1 Peter 3:15-16; 2 Timothy 2:25; Colossians 4:5-6

JUNE

Commit everything you do to the Lord. Trust him, and he will help you.

Don't worry about anything; instead, pray about everything. **Tell God what you need, and thank him for all he has done.**

Give all your worries and cares to God, for he cares about what happens to you.

Psalm 37:5; Philippians 4:6; 1 Peter 5:7

6
JUNE

Let all the world look to me for salvation! For I am God; there is no other. . . . **Every knee will bow to me, and every tongue will confess allegiance to my name.**

The people will declare, "The Lord is the source of all my righteousness and strength." And all who were angry with him will come to him and be ashamed.

Yes, each of us will have to give a personal account to God.

Isaiah 45:22-24; Romans 14:12

Be sure to do what you should, for then you will enjoy the personal satisfaction of having done your work well, and you won't need to compare yourself to anyone else.

If you wait for perfect conditions, you will never get anything done.

Be sure to stay busy and plant a variety of crops, for you never know which will grow—perhaps they all will.

It's wonderful to be young! Enjoy every minute of it. Do everything you want to do; take it all in. But remember that you must give an account to God for everything you do.

Galatians 6:4;
Ecclesiastes 11:4, 6, 9

7
JUNE

8

All of you should be of one mind, full of sympathy toward each other, loving one another with tender hearts and humble minds.

Don't repay evil for evil. Don't retaliate when people say unkind things about you. Instead, pay them back with a blessing. That is what God wants you to do, and he will bless you for it.

Be humble and gentle. Be patient with each other, making allowance for each other's faults because of your love.

1 Peter 3:8-9; Ephesians 4:2

9
JUNE

So get rid of all malicious behavior and deceit. Don't just pretend to be good! Be done with hypocrisy and jealousy and backstabbing.

Now is the time to get rid of anger, rage, malicious behavior, slander, and dirty language.

Dear friends, I am not writing a new commandment, for it is an old one you have always had, right from the beginning. This commandment—to love one another—is the same message you heard before. Yet it is also new. This commandment is true in Christ and is true among you, because the darkness is disappearing and the true light is already shining.

1 Peter 2:1; Colossians 3:8; 1 John 2:7-8

You are all children of God through faith in Christ Jesus.

For all who are led by the Spirit of God are children of God.

See how very much our heavenly Father loves us, for he allows us to be called his children, and we really are! But the people who belong to this world don't know God, so they don't understand that we are his children. Yes, dear friends, we are already God's children, and we can't even imagine what we will be like when Christ returns. But we do know that when he comes we will be like him, for we will see him as he really is.

Galatians 3:26; Romans 8:14; 1 John 3:1-2

JUNE

10

JUNE
11

His unchanging plan has always been to adopt us into his own family by bringing us to himself through Jesus Christ.

It is God who saved us and chose us to live a holy life. He did this not because we deserved it, but because that was his plan long before the world began.

You didn't choose me. **I chose you.** I appointed you to go and produce fruit that will last.

When the Holy Spirit controls our lives, he will produce this kind of fruit in us: love, joy, peace, patience, kindness, goodness, faithfulness, gentleness, and self-control.

Ephesians 1:5; 2 Timothy 1:9; John 15:16; Galatians 5:22-23

12 JUNE

Jesus was led out into the wilderness by the Holy Spirit to be tempted there by the Devil.

Even though Jesus was God's Son, he learned obedience from the things he suffered.

The temptations that come into your life are no different from what others experience. And God is faithful. He will keep the temptation from becoming so strong that you can't stand up against it.

Matthew 4:1; Hebrews 5:8; 1 Corinthians 10:13

13

Don't ignore it when the Lord disciplines you, and don't be discouraged when he corrects you.

As you endure this divine discipline, remember that God is treating you as his own children. Whoever heard of a child who was never disciplined? If God doesn't discipline you as he does all of his children, it means that you . . . are not really his children after all. Since we respect our earthly fathers who disciplined us, should we not all the more cheerfully submit to the discipline of our heavenly Father and live forever?

Proverbs 3:11; Hebrews 12:7-9

14
JUNE

I will sprinkle clean water on you, and you will be clean. . . . **And I will give you a new heart with new and right desires,** and I will put a new spirit in you. I will take out your stony heart of sin and give you a new, obedient heart.

And I will put my Spirit in you so you will obey my laws and do whatever I command.

Ezekiel 36:25-27

We know what real love is because Christ gave up his life for us.

Let us continue to love one another, for love comes from God. **Anyone who loves is born of God and knows God.**

And this is his commandment: We must believe in the name of his Son, Jesus Christ, and love one another.

1 John 3:16; 4:7; 3:23

15

16
june

The Lord is good to everyone. He showers compassion on all his creation.

He saved us, not because of the good things we did, but because of his mercy.

For this light within you produces only what is good and right and true.

Love your enemies! Pray for those who persecute you! In that way, you will be acting as true children of your Father in heaven.

Psalm 145:9; Titus 3:5; Ephesians 5:9; Matthew 5:44-45

Don't slip back into your old ways of doing evil; you didn't know any better then. But now you must be holy in everything you do, just as God—who chose you to be his children—is holy. **For he himself has said, "You must be holy because I am holy."**

For you have been born again. Your new life did not come from your earthly parents because the life they gave you will end in death. But this new life will last forever because it comes from the eternal, living word of God.

And remember that the heavenly Father to whom you pray has no favorites when he judges. He will judge or reward you according to what you do. So you must live in reverent fear of him during your time as foreigners here on earth.

1 Peter 1:14-16, 23, 17

18

JUNE

In my mind I really want to obey God's law, but because of my sinful nature I am a slave to sin.

Overwhelming victory is ours through Christ, who loved us.

Let the Lord Jesus Christ take control of you, and don't think of ways to indulge your evil desires.

Romans 7:25; 8:37; 13:14

God blesses those who are hungry and thirsty for justice, for they will receive it in full.

God blesses those who are merciful, for they will be shown mercy.

God blesses those whose hearts are pure, for they will see God.

God blesses those who work for peace, for they will be called the children of God.

Matthew 5:6-9

19 JUNE

20

Since you have heard all about him and have learned the truth that is in Jesus, throw off your old evil nature and your former way of life, which is rotten through and through, full of lust and deception.

Instead, there must be a spiritual renewal of your thoughts and attitudes.

You must display a new nature because you are a new person, created in God's likeness—righteous, holy, and true.

Ephesians 4:21-24

21 JUNE

Anna, a prophet, . . . was very old. She was a widow, for her husband had died when they had been married only seven years. She was now eighty-four years old. **She never left the Temple but stayed there day and night, worshiping God with fasting and prayer.**

A woman who is a true widow, one who is truly alone in this world, has placed her hope in God. Night and day she asks God for help and spends much time in prayer.

Praise the Lord . . . young men and maidens, old men and children. . . . For his name is very great; his glory towers over the earth and heaven!

Luke 2:36-37; 1 Timothy 5:5; Psalm 148:1, 12-13

Let us come before him with thanksgiving. Let us sing him psalms of praise. For the Lord is a great God, the great King above all gods. He owns the depths of the earth, and even the mightiest mountains are his. The sea belongs to him, for he made it. His hands formed the dry land, too.

Come, let us worship and bow down. Let us kneel before the Lord our maker, for he is our God. We are the people he watches over, the sheep under his care. Oh, that you would listen to his voice today!

Psalm 95:2-7

JUNE

JUNE
23

To whom, then, can we compare God? What image might we find to resemble him?

It is God who sits above the circle of the earth. The people below must seem to him like grasshoppers!

Look up into the heavens. Who created all the stars? He brings them out one after another, calling each by its name.

How great is our Lord! His power is absolute! His understanding is beyond comprehension!

Isaiah 40:18, 22, 26; Psalm 147:5

24 JUNE

The Lord is our God, the Lord alone. And you must love the Lord your God with all your heart, all your soul, and all your strength.

I will teach you wisdom's ways and lead you in straight paths. If you live a life guided by wisdom, you won't limp or stumble as you run.

Don't lose sight of my words. Let them penetrate deep within your heart.

Deuteronomy 6:4-5; Proverbs 4:11-12, 21

If we have hope in Christ only for this life, we are the most miserable people in the world.

But the fact is that Christ has been raised from the dead. He has become the first of a great harvest of those who will be raised to life again.

He is so rich in kindness that he purchased our freedom through the blood of his Son, and our sins are forgiven.

God paid a ransom to save you from the empty life you inherited from your ancestors. And the ransom he paid was not mere gold or silver. He paid for you with the precious lifeblood of Christ, the sinless, spotless Lamb of God.

**1 Corinthians 15:19-20; Ephesians 1:7;
1 Peter 1:18-19**

26
JUNE

He will be gentle—he will not shout or raise his voice in public. **He will not crush those who are weak or quench the smallest hope.** He will bring full justice to all who have been wronged.

He will not stop until truth and righteousness prevail throughout the earth. Even distant lands beyond the sea will wait for his instruction.

Isaiah 42:2-4

In these final days, he has spoken to us through his Son. God promised everything to the Son as an inheritance, and through the Son he made the universe and everything in it.

We will hold to the truth in love, becoming more and more in every way like Christ.

Be very careful never to forget what you have seen the Lord do for you. Do not let these things escape from your mind as long as you live!

Hebrews 1:2; Ephesians 4:15; Deuteronomy 4:9

27

28

june

Obey God because you are his children. Don't
slip back into your old ways of doing evil; you
didn't know any better then. **But now you
must be holy in everything you do, just as
God—who chose you to be his children—
is holy.**

Throw off your old evil nature. . . . There
must be a spiritual renewal of your thoughts
and attitudes. You must display a new nature
because you are a new person, created in God's
likeness—righteous, holy, and true.

1 Peter 1:14-15; Ephesians 4:22-24

JUNE 29

Keep the Sabbath day holy. Don't pursue your own interests on that day, but enjoy the Sabbath and speak of it with delight as the Lord's holy day. Honor the Lord in everything you do, and don't follow your own desires or talk idly. **If you do this, the Lord will be your delight.**

Let us not neglect our meeting together, as some people do, but encourage and warn each other, especially now that the day of his coming back again is drawing near.

Isaiah 58:13-14; Hebrews 10:25

30
JUNE

Those who can hear will listen to his voice.

Even the hotheads among them will be full of sense and understanding. Those who stammer in uncertainty will speak out plainly. **In that day ungodly fools will not be heroes**. Wealthy cheaters will not be respected as outstanding citizens. Everyone will recognize ungodly fools for what they are.

But good people will be generous to others and will be blessed for all they do.

Isaiah 32:3-6, 8

Who else can tell you what is going to happen in the days ahead? Let them tell you if they can and thus prove their power. Let them do as I have done since ancient times. . . . Is there any other God? No! **There is no other Rock—not one!**

So remember this and keep it firmly in mind: The Lord is God both in heaven and on earth, and there is no other god!

Isaiah 44:7-8; Deuteronomy 4:39

JULY

2

The law of the Lord is perfect, reviving the soul. The decrees of the Lord are trustworthy, making wise the simple. The commandments of the Lord are right, bringing joy to the heart. The commands of the Lord are clear, giving insight to life.

Meditate on [God's law] day and night so you may be sure to obey all that is written in it. Only then will you succeed. I command you—be strong and courageous! Do not be afraid or discouraged. For the Lord your God is with you wherever you go.

The Lord says, "I will guide you along the best pathway for your life."

**Psalm 19:7-8; Joshua 1:8-9;
Psalm 32:8**

3
JULY

Praise the Lord, I tell myself, and never forget the good things he does for me. He forgives all my sins and heals all my diseases. He ransoms me from death and surrounds me with love and tender mercies. **He fills my life with good things.**

What can we say about such wonderful things as these? If God is for us, who can ever be against us? Since God did not spare even his own Son but gave him up for us all, won't God, who gave us Christ, also give us everything else?

Now glory be to God! By his mighty power at work within us, he is able to accomplish infinitely more than we would ever dare to ask or hope.

**Psalm 103:2-5; Romans 8:31-32;
Ephesians 3:20**

Pray like this: Our Father in heaven, may your name be honored.

May your Kingdom come soon.

May your will be done here on earth, just as it is in heaven.

Give us our food for today, and forgive us our sins, just as we have forgiven those who have sinned against us.

And don't let us yield to temptation, but deliver us from the evil one.

Matthew 6:9-13

JULY 4

JULY
5

Put on all of God's armor so that you will be able to stand firm against all strategies and tricks of the Devil. **For we are not fighting against people made of flesh and blood, but against the evil rulers and authorities of the unseen world, against those mighty powers of darkness who rule this world, and against wicked spirits in the heavenly realms.**

Use every piece of God's armor to resist the enemy in the time of evil, so that after the battle you will still be standing firm.

Ephesians 6:11-13

6 JULY

In a race everyone runs, but only one person gets the prize. You also must run in such a way that you will win. All athletes practice strict self-control. They do it to win a prize that will fade away, but we do it for an eternal prize.

Run from all these evil things, and follow what is right and good. Pursue a godly life, along with faith, love, perseverance, and gentleness.

Fight well in the Lord's battles. **Cling tightly to your faith in Christ, and always keep your conscience clear.**

God, who began the good work within you, will continue his work until it is finally finished.

1 Corinthians 9:24-25; 1 Timothy 6:11; 1:18-19; Philippians 1:6

7

JULY

The way of the righteous is like the first gleam of dawn, which shines ever brighter until the full light of day.

No eye has seen, no ear has heard, and no mind has imagined what God has prepared for those who love him.

Take delight in the Lord, and he will give you your heart's desires. Commit everything you do to the Lord. Trust him, and he will help you.

Proverbs 4:18; 1 Corinthians 2:9; Psalm 37:4-5

8
JULY

If you are really eager to give, it isn't important how much you are able to give. God wants you to give what you have, not what you don't have.

It is possible to give freely and become more wealthy, but those who are stingy will lose everything.

Take care! **Don't do your good deeds publicly, to be admired, because then you will lose the reward from your Father in heaven.** When you give a gift to someone in need, don't shout about it.

Give your gifts in secret, and your Father, who knows all secrets, will reward you.

2 Corinthians 8:12; Proverbs 11:24; Matthew 6:1-2, 4

We know how dearly God loves us, because he has given us the Holy Spirit to fill our hearts with his love.

God showed how much he loved us by sending his only Son into the world so that we might have eternal life through him.

He is so rich in kindness that he purchased our freedom through the blood of his Son, and our sins are forgiven.

Since God loved us that much, we surely ought to love each other.

Romans 5:5; 1 John 4:9; Ephesians 1:7; 1 John 4:11

9

10

july

You have heard that the law of Moses says, "Love your neighbor" and hate your enemy. But I say, love your enemies! Pray for those who persecute you! In that way, you will be acting as true children of your Father in heaven. For he gives his sunlight to both the evil and the good, and he sends rain on the just and on the unjust, too.

If you love only those who love you, what good is that? Even corrupt tax collectors do that much.

If you are kind only to your friends, how are you different from anyone else?

Matthew 5:43-47

Christ is all that matters, and he lives in all of us.

Since God chose you to be the holy people whom he loves, you must clothe yourselves with tenderhearted mercy, kindness, humility, gentleness, and patience.

May the Lord make your love grow and overflow to each other. . . . As a result, Christ will make your hearts strong, blameless, and holy when you stand before God our Father on that day when our Lord Jesus comes.

Colossians 3:11-12; 1 Thessalonians 3:12-13

JULY 12

With this news, strengthen those who have tired hands, and encourage those who have weak knees. **Say to those who are afraid, "Be strong, and do not fear, for your God is coming to destroy your enemies. He is coming to save you."**

And when he comes, he will open the eyes of the blind and unstop the ears of the deaf. The lame will leap like a deer, and those who cannot speak will shout and sing!

Springs will gush forth in the wilderness, and streams will water the desert.

Isaiah 35:3-6

Does a farmer always plow and never sow? Is he forever cultivating the soil and never planting it? Does he not finally plant his seeds for dill, cumin, wheat, barley, and spelt, each in its own section of his land? The farmer knows just what to do, for God has given him understanding.

O Lord, what great miracles you do! And how deep are your thoughts.

You have all wisdom and do great and mighty miracles. You are very aware of the conduct of all people, and you reward them according to their deeds.

Isaiah 28:24-26; Psalm 92:5; Jeremiah 32:19

13
JULY

14

Don't worry about evil people who prosper or fret about their wicked schemes. Stop your anger! Turn from your rage! **Do not envy others—it only leads to harm.** For the wicked will be destroyed, but those who trust in the Lord will possess the land.

The way of the righteous is like the first gleam of dawn, which shines ever brighter until the full light of day.

Psalm 37:7-9; Proverbs 4:18

15 JULY

We can be mirrors that brightly reflect the glory of the Lord. And as the Spirit of the Lord works within us, we become more and more like him and reflect his glory even more.

Character strengthens our confident expectation of salvation. And this expectation will not disappoint us. For we know how dearly God loves us, because he has given us the Holy Spirit to fill our hearts with his love.

If we are living now by the Holy Spirit, let us follow the Holy Spirit's leading in every part of our lives.

2 Corinthians 3:18; Romans 5:4-5; Galatians 5:25

Remember your leaders who first taught you the word of God. Think of all the good that has come from their lives, and trust the Lord as they do.

Obey your spiritual leaders and do what they say. Their work is to watch over your souls, and they know they are accountable to God. Give them reason to do this joyfully and not with sorrow.

For wisdom is far more valuable than rubies. Nothing you desire can be compared with it.

Hebrews 13:7, 17; Proverbs 8:11

JULY

JULY
17

The laws of the Lord are true; each one is fair.
They are more desirable than gold, even the finest
gold. They are sweeter than honey, even honey
dripping from the comb. They are a warning to
those who hear them; there is great reward for
those who obey them.

**For the word of the Lord holds true, and
everything he does is worthy of our trust.** He
loves whatever is just and good, and his unfailing
love fills the earth.

Psalm 19:9-11; 33:4-5

18 JULY

This command I am giving you today is not too difficult for you to understand or perform.

But remember that the temptations that come into your life are no different from what others experience. And God is faithful. **He will keep the temptation from becoming so strong that you can't stand up against it.** When you are tempted, he will show you a way out so that you will not give in to it.

Choose to love the Lord your God and to obey him and commit yourself to him, for he is your life.

Deuteronomy 30:11; 1 Corinthians 10:13; Deuteronomy 30:20

If you try to keep your life for yourself, you will lose it. But if you give up your life for my sake and for the sake of the Good News, you will find true life.

And how do you benefit if you gain the whole world but lose your own soul in the process? Is anything worth more than your soul?

If a person is ashamed of me and my message in these adulterous and sinful days, I, the Son of Man, will be ashamed of that person when I return in the glory of my Father with the holy angels.

Mark 8:35-38

20

JULY

King Hezekiah handled the distribution throughout all Judah, doing what was pleasing and good in the sight of the Lord his God. In all that he did in the service of the Temple of God and in his efforts to follow the law and the commands, Hezekiah sought his God wholeheartedly. **As a result, he was very successful.**

Keep me from lying to myself; give me the privilege of knowing your law. I have chosen to be faithful; I have determined to live by your laws. I cling to your decrees. Lord, don't let me be put to shame!

**2 Chronicles 31:20-21;
Psalm 119:29-31**

Let us review the situation together, and you can present your case if you have one.

"Come now, let us argue this out," says the Lord. **"No matter how deep the stain of your sins, I can remove it.** I can make you as clean as freshly fallen snow."

Just think how much more the blood of Christ will purify our hearts from deeds that lead to death so that we can worship the living God. For by the power of the eternal Spirit, Christ offered himself to God as a perfect sacrifice for our sins.

Isaiah 43:26; 1:18; Hebrews 9:14

21

22
july

For if you confess with your mouth that Jesus is Lord and believe in your heart that God raised him from the dead, you will be saved. For it is by believing in your heart that you are made right with God, and it is by confessing with your mouth that you are saved. As the Scriptures tell us, **"Anyone who believes in him will not be disappointed."**

Anyone who calls on the name of the Lord will be saved.

Romans 10:9-11, 13

JULY 23

"For I know the plans I have for you," says the Lord. "They are plans for good and not for disaster, to give you a future and a hope.

"My thoughts are completely different from yours," says the Lord. "**And my ways are far beyond anything you could imagine.** For just as the heavens are higher than the earth, so are my ways higher than your ways and my thoughts higher than your thoughts.

"Come to me with your ears wide open."

Jeremiah 29:11; Isaiah 55:8-9, 3

24 JULY

When Jesus came by, he looked up at Zacchaeus and called him by name. "Zacchaeus!" he said. "Quick, come down! For I must be a guest in your home today."

Zacchaeus quickly climbed down and took Jesus to his house in great excitement and joy.

Look! Here I stand at the door and knock. If you hear me calling and open the door, I will come in, and we will share a meal as friends.

Then at last they will recognize that it is I who speaks to them.

Luke 19:5-6; Revelation 3:20; Isaiah 52:6

Love your enemies! Do good to them! Lend to them! And don't be concerned that they might not repay. Then your reward from heaven will be very great, and you will truly be acting as children of the Most High.

You must be compassionate, just as your Father is compassionate.

If you give, you will receive. Your gift will return to you in full measure, pressed down, shaken together to make room for more, and running over. Whatever measure you use in giving—large or small—it will be used to measure what is given back to you.

Luke 6:35-36, 38

25
JULY

Obey your parents because you belong to the Lord, for this is the right thing to do.

Obey your spiritual leaders and do what they say.

Submit to the government and its officers. . . . Be obedient, always ready to do what is good.

Show respect for everyone. Love your Christian brothers and sisters. Fear God. Show respect for the king.

Pray . . . for kings and all others who are in authority.

Ephesians 6:1; Hebrews 13:17; Titus 3:1; 1 Peter 2:17; 1 Timothy 2:2

27
JULY

Obey the government, for God is the one who put it there. **All governments have been placed in power by God.** So those who refuse to obey the laws of the land are refusing to obey God, and punishment will follow.

For the authorities do not frighten people who are doing right, but they frighten those who do wrong. So do what they say, and you will get along well.

Obey the government for two reasons: to keep from being punished and to keep a clear conscience.

Romans 13:1-3, 5

Get rid of all bitterness, rage, anger, harsh words, and slander, as well as all types of malicious behavior. Instead, be kind to each other, tenderhearted, forgiving one another, just as God through Christ has forgiven you.

Live a life filled with love for others, following the example of Christ, who loved you and gave himself as a sacrifice to take away your sins.

So now I am giving you a new commandment: Love each other. **Just as I have loved you, you should love each other.** Your love for one another will prove to the world that you are my disciples.

Ephesians 4:31-32; 5:2; John 13:34-35

JULY

JULY
29

You must remain faithful to the things you have been taught. . . . **You have been taught the holy Scriptures from childhood, and they have given you the wisdom to receive the salvation that comes by trusting in Christ Jesus.**

All Scripture is inspired by God and is useful to teach us what is true and to make us realize what is wrong in our lives. It straightens us out and teaches us to do what is right.

It is God's way of preparing us in every way, fully equipped for every good thing God wants us to do.

2 Timothy 3:14-17

30 JULY

So commit yourselves completely to these words of mine. Tie them to your hands as a reminder, and wear them on your forehead. **Study this Book of the Law continually.** Meditate on it day and night so you may be sure to obey all that is written in it. Only then will you succeed.

Oh, the joys of those who do not follow the advice of the wicked, or stand around with sinners, or join in with scoffers. But they delight in doing everything the Lord wants; day and night they think about his law.

Deuteronomy 11:18; Joshua 1:8; Psalm 1:1-2

Stop judging others, and you will not be judged. Stop criticizing others, or it will all come back on you. If you forgive others, you will be forgiven.

For others will treat you as you treat them.

And why worry about a speck in your friend's eye when you have a log in your own? How can you think of saying, "Let me help you get rid of that speck in your eye," when you can't see past the log in your own eye? Hypocrite! First get rid of the log from your own eye; then perhaps you will see well enough to deal with the speck in your friend's eye.

Luke 6:37; Matthew 7:2-5

1 AUGUST

Stop quarreling with God! If you agree
with him, you will have peace at last,
and things will go well for you.

You must be even more careful to
put into action God's saving work in
your lives, obeying God with deep
reverence and fear. **For God is working in you, giving you the desire to
obey him and the power to do what
pleases him.**

"For I know the plans I have for
you," says the Lord. "They are plans
for good and not for disaster."

**Job 22:21; Philippians 2:12-13;
Jeremiah 29:11**

God wants you to be holy.

In his goodness he chose to make us his own children by giving us his true word. So get rid of all the filth and evil in your lives.

[Jesus said,] "Anyone who does God's will is my brother and sister and mother.

"Anyone who listens to my teaching and obeys me is wise, like a person who builds a house on solid rock. Though the rain comes in torrents and the floodwaters rise and the winds beat against that house, it won't collapse, because it is built on rock."

1 Thessalonians 4:3; James 1:18, 21; Mark 3:35; Matthew 7:24-25

3 august

Your own actions have brought this upon you.
This punishment is a bitter dose of your own
medicine. It has pierced you to the heart!

No one has real understanding; no one is
seeking God. **All have turned away from God;
all have gone wrong.**

I know, Lord, that a person's life is not his
own. No one is able to plan his own course.
So correct me, Lord, but please be gentle.

**Jeremiah 4:18; Romans 3:11-12; Jeremiah
10:23-24**

AUGUST

God is not a man, that he should lie. He is not a human, that he should change his mind. Has he ever spoken and failed to act? Has he ever promised and not carried it through?

The Lord your God is indeed God. He is the faithful God who keeps his covenant for a thousand generations and constantly loves those who love him and obey his commands.

He always remembers his covenant.

So don't worry about tomorrow, for tomorrow will bring its own worries. Today's trouble is enough for today.

He is a mighty savior. He will rejoice over you with great gladness.

Go to God and present your case to him. For he does great works too marvelous to understand.

Numbers 23:19; Deuteronomy 7:9; Psalm 111:5; Matthew 6:34; Zephaniah 3:17; Job 5:8-9

AUGUST 5

Who has created the whole wide world?
What is his name—and his son's name?
Tell me if you know!

For the Lord is the one who shaped the
mountains, stirs up the winds, and reveals
his every thought. He turns the light of dawn
into darkness and treads the mountains
under his feet. **The Lord God Almighty is
his name!**

For the Lord is high above the nations; his
glory is far greater than the heavens. Who
can be compared with the Lord our God, who
is enthroned on high?

Proverbs 30:4; Amos 4:13; Psalm 113:4-5

The heavens tell of the glory of God. The skies display his marvelous craftsmanship.

The Lord merely spoke, and the heavens were created. He breathed the word, and all the stars were born. He gave the sea its boundaries and locked the oceans in vast reservoirs. **When he spoke, the world began!** It appeared at his command.

Who else has held the oceans in his hand? Who has measured off the heavens with his fingers? Who else knows the weight of the earth or has weighed out the mountains and the hills?

All the nations of the world are nothing in comparison with him. They are but a drop in the bucket, dust on the scales. He picks up the islands as though they had no weight at all.

Psalm 19:1; 33:6-7, 9; Isaiah 40:12, 15

6

AUGUST

7

So we are lying if we say we have fellowship with God but go on living in spiritual darkness.

And how can we be sure that we belong to him? By obeying his commandments. **If someone says, "I belong to God," but doesn't obey God's commandments, that person is a liar and does not live in the truth.** But those who obey God's word really do love him. That is the way to know whether or not we live in him. Those who say they live in God should live their lives as Christ did.

1 John 1:6; 2:3-6

8 AUGUST

Happy are people of integrity, who follow the law of the Lord. Happy are those who obey his decrees and search for him with all their hearts. They do not compromise with evil, and they walk only in his paths.

The greatest among you must be a servant. But those who exalt themselves will be humbled, and those who humble themselves will be exalted.

Psalm 119:1-3; Matthew 23:11-12

For though your hearts were once full of darkness, now you are full of light from the Lord, and your behavior should show it! For this light within you produces only what is good and right and true.

Do for others what you would like them to do for you.

Those who are honest and fair . . . will dwell on high.

Ephesians 5:8-9; Matthew 7:12; Isaiah 33:15-16

AUGUST 9

AUGUST
10

The Lord is coming soon.

In that day deaf people will hear words read from a book, and blind people will see through the gloom and darkness. The humble will be filled with fresh joy from the Lord. Those who are poor will rejoice in the Holy One of Israel. Those who intimidate and harass will be gone, and all those who plot evil will be killed.

Those in error will then believe the truth, and those who constantly complain will accept instruction.

Philippians 4:5; Isaiah 29:18-20, 24

Give what you have to anyone who asks you for it; and when things are taken away from you, don't try to get them back. Do for others as you would like them to do for you.

Do you think you deserve credit merely for loving those who love you? Even the sinners do that!

Share each other's troubles and problems, and in this way obey the law of Christ. If you think you are too important to help someone in need, you are only fooling yourself. You are really a nobody.

Luke 6:30-32; Galatians 6:2-3

12

If you give, you will receive. Your gift will return to you in full measure, pressed down, shaken together to make room for more, and running over. **Whatever measure you use in giving—large or small—it will be used to measure what is given back to you.**

Remember this—a farmer who plants only a few seeds will get a small crop. But the one who plants generously will get a generous crop.

Luke 6:38; 2 Corinthians 9:6

AUGUST

Others will treat you as you treat them.

There will be no mercy for you if you have not been merciful to others.

Stop criticizing others, or it will all come back on you. **If you forgive others, you will be forgiven.**

Keep a close watch on yourself and on your teaching. Stay true to what is right, and God will save you and those who hear you.

So see to it that you really do love each other intensely with all your hearts.

Matthew 7:2; James 2:13; Luke 6:37; 1 Timothy 4:16; 1 Peter 1:22

The tongue is a small thing, but what enormous damage it can do. A tiny spark can set a great forest on fire. **And the tongue is a flame of fire.** . . . It can turn the entire course of your life into a blazing flame of destruction. It is an uncontrollable evil, full of deadly poison.

But now is the time to get rid of anger, rage, malicious behavior, slander, and dirty language. Don't lie to each other, for you have stripped off your old evil nature and all its wicked deeds.

Some people make cutting remarks, but the words of the wise bring healing. Truth stands the test of time; lies are soon exposed.

James 3:5-6, 8; Colossians 3:8-9; Proverbs 12:18-19

14

15

august

You have heard that the law of Moses says, "If an eye is injured, injure the eye of the person who did it. If a tooth gets knocked out, knock out the tooth of the person who did it." But I say, don't resist an evil person! If you are slapped on the right cheek, turn the other, too.

A gentle answer turns away wrath, but harsh words stir up anger.

It is better to be patient than powerful; it is better to have self-control than to conquer a city.

Matthew 5:38-39; Proverbs 15:1; 16:32

You must be compassionate, just as your Father is compassionate.

Stop judging others, and you will not be judged. Stop criticizing others, or it will all come back on you. If you forgive others, you will be forgiven.

Since God chose you to be the holy people whom he loves, you must clothe yourselves with tenderhearted mercy, kindness, humility, gentleness, and patience. You must make allowance for each other's faults and forgive the person who offends you. **Remember, the Lord forgave you, so you must forgive others.** And the most important piece of clothing you must wear is love. Love is what binds us all together in perfect harmony.

Luke 6:36-37; Colossians 3:12-14

17

AUGUST

Don't try to act important, but enjoy the company of ordinary people. And don't think you know it all!

Never pay back evil for evil to anyone. Do things in such a way that everyone can see you are honorable. **Do your part to live in peace with everyone, as much as possible**.

Don't just pretend that you love others. Really love them. Hate what is wrong. Stand on the side of the good. Love each other with genuine affection, and take delight in honoring each other.

So why do you condemn another Christian? Why do you look down on another Christian? Remember, each of us will stand personally before the judgment seat of God.

Romans 12:16-18, 9-10; Romans 14:10

I don't understand myself at all, for I really want to do what is right, but I don't do it. Instead, I do the very thing I hate. I know perfectly well that what I am doing is wrong, and my bad conscience shows that I agree that the law is good.

No matter which way I turn, I can't make myself do right. I want to, but I can't.

It seems to be a fact of life that when I want to do what is right, I inevitably do what is wrong.

God is working in you, giving you the desire to obey him and the power to do what pleases him.

Romans 7:15-16, 18, 21; Philippians 2:13

18
AUGUST

19

Your new life did not come from your earthly parents because the life they gave you will end in death. But this new life will last forever because it comes from the eternal, living word of God. As the prophet says, "People are like grass that dies away; their beauty fades as quickly as the beauty of wildflowers. The grass withers, and the flowers fall away. But the word of the Lord will last forever."

Come to Christ, who is the living cornerstone of God's temple. He was rejected by the people, but he is precious to God who chose him.

1 Peter 1:23-25; 2:4

20
AUGUST

When Rehoboam was firmly established and strong, he abandoned the law of the Lord, and all Israel followed him in this sin.

He was an evil king, for he did not seek the Lord with all his heart.

I am giving you the choice between a blessing and a curse! **You will be blessed if you obey the commands of the Lord your God . . .** [but] you will receive a curse if you reject the commands of the Lord your God.

Oh, that you would choose life. . . . Choose to love the Lord your God.

2 Chronicles 12:1, 14; Deuteronomy 11:26-28; 30:19-20

Live in such a way that God's love can bless you as you wait for the eternal life that our Lord Jesus Christ in his mercy is going to give you. Show mercy to those whose faith is wavering. Rescue others by snatching them from the flames of judgment. . . . But be careful that you aren't contaminated by their sins.

[God] is able to keep you from stumbling, and . . . will bring you into his glorious presence innocent of sin and with great joy.

Jude 1:21-23, 24

AUGUST 21

AUGUST
22

If any among the people are unfaithful by consulting and following mediums or psychics, I will turn against them.

Can the living find out the future from the dead? Why not ask your God?

If we are living now by the Holy Spirit, let us follow the Holy Spirit's leading in every part of our lives.

Stand firm and keep a strong grip on everything [that has been] taught [to] you.

Leviticus 20:6; Isaiah 8:19; Galatians 5:25; 2 Thessalonians 2:15

Live no longer as the ungodly do, for they are hopelessly confused. Their closed minds are full of darkness; they are far away from the life of God because they have shut their minds and hardened their hearts against him.

But that isn't what you were taught when you learned about Christ. **Instead, there must be a spiritual renewal of your thoughts and attitudes.** You must display a new nature because you are a new person, created in God's likeness—righteous, holy, and true.

Ephesians 4:17-18, 20, 23-24

[Jesus said,] "Anyone who listens to my teaching and obeys me is wise, like a person who builds a house on solid rock. Though the rain comes in torrents and the flood-waters rise and the winds beat against that house, it won't collapse, because it is built on rock.

"But anyone who hears my teaching and ignores it is foolish, like a person who builds a house on sand. When the rains and floods come and the winds beat against that house, it will fall with a mighty crash."

The crowds were amazed at [Jesus'] teaching, for he taught as one who had real authority.

Matthew 7:24-29

25

AUGUST

It was by faith that Moses, when he grew up, refused to be treated as the son of Pharaoh's daughter. **He chose to share the oppression of God's people instead of enjoying the fleeting pleasures of sin.** He thought it was better to suffer for the sake of the Messiah than to own the treasures of Egypt, for he was looking ahead to the great reward that God would give him.

It was by faith that Moses left the land of Egypt. He was not afraid of the king. Moses kept right on going because he kept his eyes on the one who is invisible.

Hebrews 11:24-27

It would take too long to recount the stories of the faith of Gideon, Barak, Samson, Jephthah, David, Samuel, and all the prophets.

By faith these people overthrew kingdoms, ruled with justice, and received what God had promised them. They shut the mouths of lions, quenched the flames of fire, and escaped death by the edge of the sword. Their weakness was turned to strength. They became strong in battle and put whole armies to flight.

Hebrews 11:32-34

26

27

august

These are the words [David] sang: "The Lord is my rock, my fortress, and my savior; my God is my rock, in whom I find protection. He is my shield, the strength of my salvation, and my stronghold, my high tower, my savior, the one who saves me from violence."

The Lord is my strength, my shield from every danger. I trust in him with all my heart. He helps me, and my heart is filled with joy.

That is why we can say with confidence, "The Lord is my helper, so I will not be afraid. What can mere mortals do to me?"

2 Samuel 22:2-3; Psalm 28:7; Hebrews 13:6

AUGUST 28

Two of the men who had explored the land, Joshua
. . . and Caleb . . . said to the community of Israel,
"The land we explored is a wonderful land! **And
if the Lord is pleased with us, he will bring us
safely into that land and give it to us.** It is a rich
land flowing with milk and honey, and he will give it
to us! Do not rebel against the Lord, and don't be
afraid of the people of the land."

But the whole community began to talk about
stoning Joshua and Caleb.

Now, who will want to harm you if you are
eager to do good? But even if you suffer for
doing what is right, God will reward you for it.
So don't be afraid and don't worry. Instead, you
must worship Christ as Lord of your life.

Numbers 14:6-10; 1 Peter 3:13-15

29
AUGUST

Jesus . . . looked up to heaven and said, "Father."

You are all children of God through faith in Christ Jesus.

And because you . . . have become his children, **God has sent the Spirit of his Son into your hearts, and now you can call God your dear Father.**

So you should not be like cowering, fearful slaves. You should behave instead like God's very own children.

[God] will welcome you . . . and . . . be your Father, and you will be [his] sons and daughters.

John 17:1; Galatians 3:26; 4:6; Romans 8:15; 2 Corinthians 6:17-18

There are many parts, but only one body.

Now all of you together are Christ's body, and each one of you is a separate and necessary part of it.

Don't let anyone think less of you because you are young. Be an example to all believers in what you teach, in the way you live, in your love, your faith, and your purity.

It is the same Lord we are serving.

**1 Corinthians 12:20, 27;
1 Timothy 4:12; 1 Corinthians 12:5**

30
AUGUST

31

AUGUST

Since God in his wisdom saw to it that the world would never find him through human wisdom, he has used our foolish preaching to save all who believe.

God's way seems foolish to the Jews because they want a sign from heaven to prove it is true. And it is foolish to the Greeks because they believe only what agrees with their own wisdom.

God alone made it possible for you to be in Christ Jesus. **For our benefit God made Christ to be wisdom itself.** He is the one who made us acceptable to God. He made us pure and holy, and he gave himself to purchase our freedom.

1 Corinthians 1:21-22, 30

1
SEPTEMBER

Obey your parents because you belong to the Lord, for this is the right thing to do. "Honor your father and mother." This is the first of the Ten Commandments that ends with a promise. And this is the promise: **If you honor your father and mother, "you will live a long life, full of blessing."**

Keep their words always in your heart. Tie them around your neck.

What you learn from them will crown you with grace and clothe you with honor.

Ephesians 6:1-3; Proverb 6:21; Proverb 1:9

Oh, the joys of those who do not follow the advice of the wicked, or stand around with sinners, or join in with scoffers.

But they delight in doing everything the Lord wants; day and night they think about his law.

They are like trees planted along the riverbank, bearing fruit each season without fail. Their leaves never wither, and in all they do, they prosper.

Psalm 1:1-3

SEPTEMBER

2

SEPTEMBER
3

Cursed are those who put their trust in mere humans and turn their hearts away from the Lord. They are like stunted shrubs in the desert, with no hope for the future. They will live in the barren wilderness, on the salty flats where no one lives.

But blessed are those who trust in the Lord and have made the Lord their hope and confidence. They are like trees planted along a riverbank, with roots that reach deep into the water. Such trees are not bothered by the heat or worried by long months of drought. Their leaves stay green, and they go right on producing delicious fruit.

Jeremiah 17:5-8

4 SEPTEMBER

Peter went over the side of the boat and walked on the water toward Jesus. But when he looked around at the high waves, he was terrified and began to sink. "Save me, Lord!" he shouted. Instantly Jesus reached out his hand and grabbed him.

O Lord God Almighty! **Where is there anyone as mighty as you, Lord?** . . . You are the one who rules the oceans. When their waves rise in fearful storms, you subdue them.

Mightier than the violent raging of the seas, mightier than the breakers on the shore—the Lord above is mightier than these!

Matthew 14:29-31; Psalm 89:8-9; 93:4

5

Can anything ever separate us from Christ's love? Does it mean he no longer loves us if we have trouble or calamity, or are persecuted, or are hungry or cold or in danger or threatened with death?

I am convinced that nothing can ever separate us from his love. Death can't, and life can't. The angels can't, and the demons can't. **Our fears for today, our worries about tomorrow, even the powers of hell can't keep God's love away.** Whether we are high above the sky or in the deepest ocean, nothing in all creation will ever be able to separate us from the love of God that is revealed in Christ Jesus our Lord.

Romans 8:35, 38-39

6
SEPTEMBER

The Lord is my rock, my fortress, and my savior; my God is my rock, in whom I find protection. He is my shield, the strength of my salvation, and my stronghold.

As for God, his way is perfect. **All the Lord's promises prove true.** He is a shield for all who look to him for protection. For who is God except the Lord? Who but our God is a solid rock?

Psalm 18:2, 30-31

The Lord is my shepherd; I have everything I need. He lets me rest in green meadows; he leads me beside peaceful streams. He renews my strength. **He guides me along right paths, bringing honor to his name**.

Even when I walk through the dark valley of death, I will not be afraid, for you are close beside me. Your rod and your staff protect and comfort me.

You prepare a feast for me in the presence of my enemies. You welcome me as a guest, anointing my head with oil. My cup overflows with blessings. Surely your goodness and unfailing love will pursue me all the days of my life, and I will live in the house of the Lord forever.

Psalm 23:1-6

SEPTEMBER

7

8

september

From the time the world was created, people have seen the earth and sky and all that God made. They can clearly see his invisible qualities—his eternal power and divine nature. So they have no excuse whatsoever for not knowing God.

When I look at the night sky and see the work of your fingers—the moon and the stars you have set in place—what are mortals that you should think of us, mere humans that you should care for us?

Day after day [the heavens] continue to speak; night after night they make him known. They speak without a sound or a word; their voice is silent in the skies; yet their message has gone out to all the earth, and their words to all the world. The sun lives in the heavens where God placed it.

Those who are wise will shine as bright as the sky, and those who turn many to righteousness will shine like stars forever.

Romans 1:20; Psalm 8:3-4; 19:2-4; Daniel 12:3

SEPTEMBER

9

The earth is the Lord's, and everything in it. The world and all its people belong to him. For he laid the earth's foundation on the seas and built it on the ocean depths.

Who may climb the mountain of the Lord? Who may stand in his holy place? Only those whose hands and hearts are pure, who do not worship idols and never tell lies. They will receive the Lord's blessing and have right standing with God their savior. They alone may enter God's presence and worship the God of Israel.

Psalm 24:1-6

10

SEPTEMBER

The Lord sent poisonous snakes among [the people of Israel], and many of them were bitten and died. Then the people came to Moses and cried out, "We have sinned."

Then the Lord told him, "Make a replica of a poisonous snake and attach it to the top of a pole. Those who are bitten will live if they simply look at it!"

And as Moses lifted up the bronze snake on a pole in the wilderness, so I [Jesus], the Son of Man, must be lifted up on a pole, so that everyone who believes in me will have eternal life.

Numbers 21:6-8; John 3:14-15

All have turned away from God; all have gone wrong. No one does good, not even one.

All have sinned; all fall short of God's glorious standard. **Yet now God in his gracious kindness declares us not guilty.** He has done this through Christ Jesus, who has freed us by taking away our sins.

Who then will condemn us?

Romans 3:12, 23-24; 8:34

SEPTEMBER

12

His unchanging plan has always been to adopt us into his own family by bringing us to himself through Jesus Christ. **And this gave him great pleasure.**

He is so rich in kindness that he purchased our freedom through the blood of his Son, and our sins are forgiven. He has showered his kindness on us, along with all wisdom and understanding.

Ephesians 1:5, 7-8

13
SEPTEMBER

We love each other as a result of his loving us first.

We know how much God loves us, and we have put our trust in him. **God is love, and all who live in love live in God, and God lives in them.**

Most important of all, continue to show deep love for each other, for love covers a multitude of sins.

Live a life filled with love for others, following the example of Christ, who loved you and gave himself as a sacrifice to take away your sins.

1 John 4:19, 16; 1 Peter 4:8; Ephesians 5:2

Let us continue to love one another, for love comes from God. Anyone who loves is born of God and knows God. But anyone who does not love does not know God—for God is love.

God showed how much he loved us by sending his only Son into the world so that we might have eternal life through him. This is real love. It is not that we loved God, but that he loved us and sent his Son as a sacrifice to take away our sins.

Since God loved us that much, we surely ought to love each other.

1 John 4:7-11

SEPTEMBER
14

SEPTEMBER
15

Accept Christians who are weak in faith, and don't argue with them about what they think is right or wrong.

Live in harmony with each other. **Don't try to act important.**

When others are happy, be happy with them. If they are sad, share their sorrow.

Romans 14:1; 12:16, 15

My dear brothers and sisters, how can you claim that you have faith in our glorious Lord Jesus Christ if you favor some people more than others?

For instance, suppose someone comes into your meeting dressed in fancy clothes and expensive jewelry, and another comes in who is poor and dressed in shabby clothes. If you give special attention and a good seat to the rich person, but you say to the poor one, "You can stand over there, or else sit on the floor"—well, doesn't this discrimination show that you are guided by wrong motives?

James 2:1-4

God is both kind and severe. He is severe to those who disobeyed, but kind to you as you continue to trust in his kindness.

O Lord, come back to us! How long will you delay? Take pity on your servants! **Satisfy us in the morning with your unfailing love, so we may sing for joy to the end of our lives.**

Teach us to make the most of our time, so that we may grow in wisdom.

Romans 11:22; Psalm 90:13-14, 12

18
SEPTEMBER

The Lord is coming soon.

In that day the wolf and the lamb will live together; the leopard and the goat will be at peace. **Calves and yearlings will be safe among lions, and a little child will lead them all.**

The cattle will graze among bears. Cubs and calves will lie down together. And lions will eat grass as the livestock do.

Babies will crawl safely among poisonous snakes. Yes, a little child will put its hand in a nest of deadly snakes and pull it out unharmed.

Philippians 4:5; Isaiah 11:6-8

People are like grass that dies away; their beauty fades as quickly as the beauty of wildflowers. The grass withers, and the flowers fall away. But the word of the Lord will last forever.

The word of God is full of living power. It is sharper than the sharpest knife, cutting deep into our innermost thoughts and desires. It exposes us for what we really are.

All Scripture is inspired by God and is useful to teach us what is true and to make us realize what is wrong in our lives. It straightens us out and teaches us to do what is right.

1 Peter 1:24-25; Hebrews 4:12; 2 Timothy 3:16

19

20

september

Learn the meaning of this Scripture: "I want you to be merciful; I don't want your sacrifices." For I have come to call sinners, not those who think they are already good enough.

Oh, that we might know the Lord! Let us press on to know him! Then he will respond to us as surely as the arrival of dawn or the coming of rains in early spring.

God blesses those who are hungry and thirsty for justice, for they will receive it in full.

Matthew 9:13; Hosea 6:3; Matthew 5:6

Everything is pure to those whose hearts are pure. But nothing is pure to those who are corrupt and unbelieving, because their minds and consciences are defiled.

Such people claim they know God, but they deny him by the way they live. They are despicable and disobedient, worthless for doing anything good.

But as for you, promote the kind of living that reflects right teaching.

Titus 1:15-16; 2:1

SEPTEMBER 22

Knowing God leads to self-control. Self-control leads to patient endurance, and patient endurance leads to godliness. Godliness leads to love for other Christians, and finally you will grow to have genuine love for everyone. **The more you grow like this, the more you will become productive and useful in your knowledge of our Lord Jesus Christ.**

Work hard to prove that you really are among those God has called and chosen. Doing this, you will never stumble or fall away. And God will open wide the gates of heaven for you to enter into the eternal Kingdom of our Lord and Savior Jesus Christ.

2 Peter 1:6-8, 10-11

Don't let the excitement of youth cause you to forget your Creator. Honor him in your youth before you grow old and no longer enjoy living. It will be too late then to remember him, when the light of the sun and moon and stars is dim to your old eyes, and there is no silver lining left among the clouds. Your limbs will tremble with age, and your strong legs will grow weak. Your teeth will be too few to do their work, and you will be blind, too. Even the chirping of birds will wake you up. But you yourself will be deaf and tuneless, with a quavering voice.

Yes, remember your Creator now while you are young.

Ecclesiastes 12:1-4, 6

23

SEPTEMBER

24

Bring your petitions, and return to the Lord. Say to him, "Forgive all our sins and graciously receive us, so that we may offer you the sacrifice of praise."

There is salvation in no one else! There is no other name in all of heaven for people to call on to save them.

We are made right in God's sight when we trust in Jesus Christ to take away our sins. And we all can be saved in this same way, no matter who we are or what we have done.

We are made right with God through faith and not by obeying the law.

Hosea 14:2; Acts 4:12; Romans 3:22, 28

25
SEPTEMBER

Jesus called a small child over to him and put the child among them.

Then he said, "I assure you, unless you turn from your sins and become as little children, you will never get into the Kingdom of Heaven. **Therefore, anyone who becomes as humble as this little child is the greatest in the Kingdom of Heaven.**

"Beware that you don't despise a single one of these little ones. For I tell you that in heaven their angels are always in the presence of my heavenly Father."

Matthew 18:2-4, 10

Peacemakers will plant seeds of peace and reap a harvest of goodness.

Let us follow the Holy Spirit's leading in every part of our lives. Let us not become conceited, or irritate one another, or be jealous of one another.

Cling tightly to your faith in Christ, and always keep your conscience clear.

James 3:18; Galatians 5:25-26; 1 Timothy 1:19

SEPTEMBER 26

SEPTEMBER
27

It is by our actions that we know we are living in the truth, so we will be confident when we stand before the Lord, even if our hearts condemn us. For God is greater than our hearts, and he knows everything.

If our conscience is clear, we can come to God with bold confidence. And we will receive whatever we request because we obey him and do the things that please him. And this is his commandment: We must believe in the name of his Son, Jesus Christ, and love one another.

1 John 3:19-23

28 SEPTEMBER

A young woman named Rebekah arrived with a water jug on her shoulder. . . . She went down to the spring, filled her jug, and came up again. Running over to her, the servant asked, "Please give me a drink."

"Certainly, sir," she said, and she quickly lowered the jug for him to drink. When he had finished, she said, "I'll draw water for your camels, too, until they have had enough!" So she quickly emptied the jug into the watering trough and ran down to the well again. She kept carrying water to the camels until they had finished drinking. Then at last, when the camels had finished drinking, he gave her a gold ring for her nose and two large gold bracelets for her wrists.

Work hard and cheerfully at whatever you do, as though you were working for the Lord.

If you give, you will receive.

Genesis 24:15-20, 22; Colossians 3:23; Luke 6:38

Don't get involved in foolish, ignorant arguments that only start fights. The Lord's servants must not quarrel but must be kind to everyone.

Do your part to live in peace with everyone, as much as possible.

If you are slapped on the right cheek, turn the other, too.

You have heard that the law of Moses says, "Love your neighbor" and hate your enemy. But I [Jesus] say, love your enemies! Pray for those who persecute you! In that way, you will be acting as true children of your Father in heaven.

2 Timothy 2:23-24; Romans 12:18; Matthew 5:39, 43-45

30
SEPTEMBER

If you are bitterly jealous and there is selfish ambition in your hearts, don't brag about being wise. That is the worst kind of lie. For jealousy and selfishness are not God's kind of wisdom. Such things are earthly, unspiritual, and motivated by the Devil. **For wherever there is jealousy and selfish ambition, there you will find disorder and every kind of evil.**

But the wisdom that comes from heaven is first of all pure. It is also peace loving, gentle at all times, and willing to yield to others. It is full of mercy and good deeds. And those who are peacemakers will plant seeds of peace and reap a harvest of goodness.

James 3:14-18

Who will want to harm you if you are eager to do good? But even if you suffer for doing what is right, God will reward you for it. So don't be afraid and don't worry. Instead, you must worship Christ as Lord of your life. **And if you are asked about your Christian hope, always be ready to explain it.** But you must do this in a gentle and respectful way.

Keep your conscience clear. Then if people speak evil against you, they will be ashamed when they see what a good life you live because you belong to Christ. Remember, it is better to suffer for doing good, if that is what God wants, than to suffer for doing wrong!

1 Peter 3:13-17

october 2

If people persecute you because you are a Christian, don't curse them; pray that God will bless them.

Don't say, "Now I can pay them back for all their meanness to me!"

Stay away from complaining and arguing, so that no one can speak a word of blame against you.

Let us continue to love one another.

Romans 12:14; Proverbs 24:29; Philippians 2:14-15; 1 John 4:7

OCTOBER

The Lord came down in a pillar of cloud and called out his own name, "the Lord," as Moses stood there in his presence. **He passed in front of Moses and said, "I am the Lord, I am the Lord, the merciful and gracious God.** I am slow to anger and rich in unfailing love and faithfulness."

Follow God's example in everything you do, because you are his dear children.

When the Holy Spirit controls our lives, he will produce this kind of fruit in us: love, joy, peace, patience, kindness, goodness, faithfulness, gentleness, and self-control.

Don't let the sun go down while you are still angry, for anger gives a mighty foothold to the Devil.

**Exodus 34:5-6; Ephesians 5:1;
Galatians 5:22-23; Ephesians 4:26-27**

OCTOBER 4

Though your hearts were once full of darkness, now you are full of light from the Lord, and your behavior should show it! **For this light within you produces only what is good and right and true.**

Try to find out what is pleasing to the Lord. Take no part in the worthless deeds of evil and darkness; instead, rebuke and expose them.

When the light shines on them, it becomes clear how evil these things are.

Ephesians 5:8-11, 13

You have stripped off your old evil nature and all its wicked deeds. **In its place you have clothed yourselves with a brand-new nature that is continually being renewed as you learn more and more about Christ, who created this new nature within you.**

Since God chose you to be the holy people whom he loves, you must clothe yourselves with tenderhearted mercy, kindness, humility, gentleness, and patience.

Colossians 3:9-10, 12

OCTOBER 5

6

Those who control their tongues can also control themselves in every other way. We can make a large horse turn around and go wherever we want by means of a small bit in its mouth. And a tiny rudder makes a huge ship turn wherever the pilot wants it to go, even though the winds are strong.

So also, the tongue is a small thing, but what enormous damage it can do. A tiny spark can set a great forest on fire. And the tongue is a flame of fire. It is full of wickedness that can ruin your whole life. It can turn the entire course of your life into a blazing flame of destruction, for it is set on fire by hell itself.

James 3:2-6

7
OCTOBER

The Lord will work out his plans for my life—for your faithful love, O Lord, endures forever. Don't abandon me, for you made me.

How precious are your thoughts about me, O God! They are innumerable! I can't even count them; they outnumber the grains of sand! **And when I wake up in the morning, you are still with me!**

Search me, O God, and know my heart; test me and know my thoughts. Point out anything in me that offends you, and lead me along the path of everlasting life.

Psalm 138:8; 139:17-18, 23-24

God blesses the people who patiently endure testing. Afterward they will receive the crown of life that God has promised to those who love him.

And remember, no one who wants to do wrong should ever say, "God is tempting me." God is never tempted to do wrong, and he never tempts anyone else either. **Temptation comes from the lure of our own evil desires.** These evil desires lead to evil actions, and evil actions lead to death. So don't be misled, my dear brothers and sisters.

Whatever is good and perfect comes to us from God above, who created all heaven's lights. Unlike them, he never changes or casts shifting shadows.

James 1:12-17

OCTOBER

8

OCTOBER
9

Who is the great liar? The one who says that Jesus is not the Christ. Such people are antichrists, for they have denied the Father and the Son.

Many deceivers have gone out into the world. They do not believe that Jesus Christ came to earth in a real body. . . . Watch out, so that you do not lose the prize for which we have been working so hard. Be diligent so that you will receive your full reward.

Do not throw away this confident trust in the Lord, no matter what happens. Remember the great reward it brings you!

1 John 2:22; 2 John 1:7-8; Hebrews 10:35

God so loved the world that he gave his only Son, so that everyone who believes in him will not perish but have eternal life.
Those who do not trust him have already been judged for not believing in the only Son of God. Their judgment is based on this fact: The light from heaven came into the world, but they loved the darkness more than the light, for their actions were evil.
But those who do what is right come to the light gladly, so everyone can see that they are doing what God wants.

John 3:16, 18-19, 21

We can be mirrors that brightly reflect the glory of the Lord. And as the Spirit of the Lord works within us, we become more and more like him.

For God knew his people in advance, and he chose them to become like his Son. . . . And having chosen them, he called them to come to him. And he gave them right standing with himself, and he promised them his glory.

[Become] more and more in every way like Christ.

2 Corinthians 3:18; Romans 8:29-30; Ephesians 4:15

12
OCTOBER

Don't copy the behavior and customs of this world, but let God transform you into a new person by changing the way you think.

You have clothed yourselves with a brand-new nature that is continually being renewed as you learn more and more about Christ, who created this new nature within you.

You must display a new nature because you are a new person, created in God's likeness— righteous, holy, and true.

Romans 12:2; Colossians 3:10; Ephesians 4:24

So get rid of all malicious behavior and deceit. Don't just pretend to be good! Be done with hypocrisy and jealousy and backstabbing.

You must crave pure spiritual milk so that you can grow into the fullness of your salvation. Cry out for this nourishment as a baby cries for milk, now that you have had a taste of the Lord's kindness. Come to Christ, who is the living cornerstone of God's temple. He was rejected by the people, but he is precious to God who chose him.

And now God is building you, as living stones, into his spiritual temple.

1 Peter 2:1-5

13

14

october

At the name of Jesus every knee will bow, in heaven and on earth and under the earth, and every tongue will confess that Jesus Christ is Lord, to the glory of God the Father.

All kings will bow before him, and all nations will serve him.

The Lord is king! He is robed in majesty. Indeed, the Lord is robed in majesty and armed with strength.

He displays his power in the whirlwind and the storm. The billowing clouds are the dust beneath his feet.

Philippians 2:10-11; Psalm 72:11; 93:1; Nahum 1:3

When Bartimaeus heard that Jesus from Nazareth was nearby, he began to shout out, "Jesus, Son of David, have mercy on me!"

When Jesus heard him, he stopped and said, "Tell him to come here."

So they called the blind man. "Cheer up," they said. "Come on, he's calling you!"

"Teacher," the blind man said, "I want to see!"

And Jesus said to him, "Go your way. Your faith has healed you." And instantly the blind man could see! Then he followed Jesus down the road.

Jesus Christ is the same yesterday, today, and forever.

Mark 10:47, 49, 51-52; Hebrews 13:8

16
OCTOBER

Long ago, even before he made the world, God loved us and chose us in Christ to be holy and without fault in his eyes. His unchanging plan has always been to adopt us into his own family by bringing us to himself through Jesus Christ. And this gave him great pleasure.

For we are God's masterpiece. He has created us anew in Christ Jesus, so that we can do the good things he planned for us long ago.

Ephesians 1:4-5; 2:10

Keep me from lying to myself; give me the privilege of knowing your law. . . . I cling to your decrees. Lord, don't let me be put to shame! If you will help me, I will run to follow your commands.

Teach me, O Lord, to follow every one of your principles. Give me understanding and I will obey your law; I will put it into practice with all my heart. Make me walk along the path of your commands, for that is where my happiness is found.

Psalm 119:29-35

17
OCTOBER

18

If you find [wisdom], you will have a bright future, and your hopes will not be cut short.

Cry out for insight and understanding. Search for them as you would for lost money or hidden treasure. Then you will understand what it means to fear the Lord, and you will gain knowledge of God.

For the Lord grants wisdom! From his mouth come knowledge and understanding.

Proverbs 24:14; Proverbs 2:3-6

19
OCTOBER

There is no one like the God of Israel. He rides across the heavens to help you. **The eternal God is your refuge, and his everlasting arms are under you.**

His brilliant splendor fills the heavens, and the earth is filled with his praise! What a wonderful God he is!

Deuteronomy 33:26-27; Habakkuk 3:3

Rejoice greatly, O people of Zion! Shout in triumph, O people of Jerusalem! Look, your king is coming to you. He is righteous and victorious, yet he is humble.

The Lord . . . will rescue his people, just as a shepherd rescues his sheep. They will sparkle in his land like jewels in a crown. How wonderful and beautiful they will be!

The young men and women will thrive on the abundance of grain and new wine.

Zechariah 9:9, 16-17

OCTOBER
20

OCTOBER
21

If you are asked about your Christian hope, always be ready to explain it.

Go into all the world and preach the Good News to everyone, everywhere.

It is the power of God at work, saving everyone who believes.

You are generous because of your faith. And I am praying that you will really put your generosity to work, for in so doing you will come to an understanding of all the good things we can do for Christ.

1 Peter 3:15; Mark 16:15; Romans 1:16; Philemon 1:6

Abraham . . . suddenly noticed three men standing nearby. He got up and ran to meet them, welcoming them by bowing low to the ground. "My lord," he said, "if it pleases you, stop here for a while. Rest in the shade of this tree while my servants get some water to wash your feet. Let me prepare some food to refresh you. . . ."

So Abraham ran back to the tent and said to Sarah, "Quick! Get three measures of your best flour, and bake some bread."

Don't forget to show hospitality to strangers, for some who have done this have entertained angels without realizing it!

Genesis 18:1-6; Hebrews 13:2

We are not our own masters when we live or when we die.

I advise you to live according to your new life in the Holy Spirit. Then you won't be doing what your sinful nature craves. **The old sinful nature loves to do evil, which is just opposite from what the Holy Spirit wants.**

[God] will keep the temptation from becoming so strong that you can't stand up against it.

Romans 14:7; Galatians 5:16-17; 1 Corinthians 10:13

24

OCTOBER

Jesus was led out into the wilderness by the Holy Spirit to be tempted there by the Devil.

God is faithful. **He will keep the temptation from becoming so strong that you can't stand up against it.** When you are tempted, he will show you a way out so that you will not give in to it.

Since he himself has gone through suffering and temptation, he is able to help us when we are being tempted.

Matthew 4:1; 1 Corinthians 10:13; Hebrews 2:18

When God saw that [the people of Nineveh] had put a stop to their evil ways, he had mercy on them and didn't carry out the destruction he had threatened.

This change of plans upset Jonah, and he became very angry.

Destruction is certain for those who argue with their Creator. Does a clay pot ever argue with its maker? Does the clay dispute with the one who shapes it, saying, "Stop, you are doing it wrong!" Does the pot exclaim, "How clumsy can you be!"

Jonah 3:10; 4:1; Isaiah 45:9

25

26

october

My dear brothers and sisters, be quick to listen, slow to speak, and slow to get angry.

It is better to be patient than powerful; it is better to have self-control than to conquer a city.

We all make many mistakes, but those who control their tongues can also control themselves in every other way.

Take control of what I say, O Lord, and keep my lips sealed.

James 1:19; Proverbs 16:32; James 3:2; Psalm 141:3

You chart the path ahead of me and tell me where to stop and rest. Every moment you know where I am. **You know what I am going to say even before I say it, Lord.**

If I go up to heaven, you are there; if I go down to the place of the dead, you are there. If I ride the wings of the morning, if I dwell by the farthest oceans, even there your hand will guide me, and your strength will support me.

Psalm 139:3-4, 8-10

28

OCTOBER

Praise the name of God forever and ever, for he alone has all wisdom and power. **He determines the course of world events; he removes kings and sets others on the throne.** He gives wisdom to the wise and knowledge to the scholars. He reveals deep and mysterious things and knows what lies hidden in darkness, though he himself is surrounded by light.

Daniel 2:20-22

Grow in the special favor and knowledge of our Lord and Savior Jesus Christ.

We can be mirrors that brightly reflect the glory of the Lord. And as the Spirit of the Lord works within us, we become more and more like him.

As we live in God, our love grows more perfect. So we will not be afraid on the day of judgment, but we can face him with confidence because we are like Christ here in this world.

2 Peter 3:18; 2 Corinthians 3:18; 1 John 4:17

29
OCTOBER

30

When you pray, don't babble on and on as people of other religions do. They think their prayers are answered only by repeating their words again and again. Don't be like them, because your Father knows exactly what you need even before you ask him!

But when you pray, go away by yourself, shut the door behind you, and pray to your Father secretly. Then your Father, who knows all secrets, will reward you.

Matthew 6:7-8, 6

"How shall I describe this generation?" Jesus asked. "With what will I compare them? They are like a group of children playing a game in the public square. They complain to their friends, 'We played wedding songs, and you weren't happy, so we played funeral songs, but you weren't sad.'

"John the Baptist didn't drink wine and he often fasted, and [the Pharisees] say, 'He's demon possessed.' And I, the Son of Man, feast and drink, and [the Pharisees] say, 'He's a glutton and a drunkard, and a friend of the worst sort of sinners!'

"I have come to call sinners, not those who think they are already good enough."

Luke 7:31-34; Matthew 9:13

All have sinned; all fall short of God's glorious standard. Yet now God in his gracious kindness declares us not guilty. He has done this through Christ Jesus, who has freed us by taking away our sins. **For God sent Jesus to take the punishment for our sins and to satisfy God's anger against us.** We are made right with God when we believe that Jesus shed his blood, sacrificing his life for us.

For God so loved the world that he gave his only Son, so that everyone who believes in him will not perish but have eternal life.

Romans 3:23-25; John 3:16

NOVEMBER 1

NOVEMBER
2

"Come now, let us argue this out," says the Lord.
"No matter how deep the stain of your sins, I can
remove it. I can make you as clean as freshly
fallen snow. Even if you are stained as red as
crimson, I can make you as white as wool."

You belong to Christ Jesus. Though you
once were far away from God, now you have
been brought near to him because of the blood
of Christ.

Isaiah 1:18; Ephesians 2:13

3 NOVEMBER

Don't worry about tomorrow, for tomorrow will bring its own worries. **Today's trouble is enough for today.**

Trust in the Lord with all your heart; do not depend on your own understanding. Seek his will in all you do, and he will direct your paths.

Give all your worries and cares to God, for he cares about what happens to you.

Matthew 6:34; Proverbs 3:5-6; 1 Peter 5:7

The Lord is good. When trouble comes, he is a strong refuge.

So we will not fear, even if earthquakes come and the mountains crumble into the sea.

The Lord is slow to get angry, but his power is great, and he never lets the guilty go unpunished. He displays his power in the whirlwind and the storm. The billowing clouds are the dust beneath his feet. In his presence the mountains quake, and the hills melt away; the earth trembles, and its people are destroyed.

The Lord saves the godly; he is their fortress in times of trouble.

Nahum 1:7; Psalm 46:2; Nahum 1:3, 5; Psalm 37:39

5 NOVEMBER

God made the earth by his power, and he preserves it by his wisdom. He has stretched out the heavens by his understanding.

When he speaks, there is thunder in the heavens. He causes the clouds to rise over the earth. He sends the lightning with the rain and releases the wind from his storehouses.

Lord, there is no one like you! For you are great, and your name is full of power.

Jeremiah 10:12-13, 6

[Sailors], too, observed the Lord's power in action, his impressive works on the deepest seas. He spoke, and the winds rose, stirring up the waves. Their ships were tossed to the heavens and sank again to the depths; the sailors cringed in terror. They reeled and staggered like drunkards and were at their wits' end.

"Lord, help!" they cried in their trouble, and he saved them from their distress. He calmed the storm to a whisper and stilled the waves.

What a blessing was that stillness as he brought them safely into harbor!

Psalm 107:24-30

november

Can a mother forget her nursing child? Can she feel no love for a child she has borne? But even if that were possible, I would not forget you!

The steps of the godly are directed by the Lord. He delights in every detail of their lives.

The Lord's delight is in those who honor him, those who put their hope in his unfailing love.

I will put my laws in their minds, and I will write them on their hearts. I will be their God, and they will be my people.

Isaiah 49:15; Psalm 37:23; 147:11; Jeremiah 31:33

NOVEMBER

8

Those who feared the Lord spoke with each other, and the Lord listened to what they said. In his presence, a scroll of remembrance was written to record the names of those who feared him and loved to think about him. **"They will be my people,"** says the Lord Almighty. **"On the day when I act, they will be my own special treasure."**

You will go free, leaping with joy like calves let out to pasture.

Malachi 3:16-17; 4:2

NOVEMBER 9

All athletes practice strict self-control. They do it to win a prize that will fade away, but we do it for an eternal prize.

Let us strip off every weight that slows us down, especially the sin that so easily hinders our progress. **And let us run with endurance the race that God has set before us.**

We do this by keeping our eyes on Jesus, on whom our faith depends from start to finish.

1 Corinthians 9:25; Hebrews 12:1-2

He . . . made the world and everything in it. Since he is Lord of heaven and earth, he doesn't live in man-made temples, and human hands can't serve his needs—for he has no needs. **He himself gives life and breath to everything, and he satisfies every need there is.**

He is not far from any one of us. For in him we live and move and exist.

Acts 17:24-25, 27-28

NOVEMBER 10

A messenger soon arrived in Jerusalem to tell King David, "All Israel has joined Absalom in a conspiracy against you!"

I [Jeremiah] have heard the many rumors about me. . . . They say, "If you say anything, we will report it." Even my old friends are watching me, waiting for a fatal slip.

But God is my helper. The Lord is the one who keeps me alive!

The Lord stands beside me like a great warrior.

2 Samuel 15:13; Jeremiah 20:10; Psalm 54:4; Jeremiah 20:11

12
NOVEMBER

Pray for the happiness of those who curse you.
Pray for those who hurt you. If someone slaps
you on one cheek, turn the other cheek. If someone demands your coat, offer your shirt also.
**Give what you have to anyone who asks you
for it;** and when things are taken away from
you, don't try to get them back. Do for others
as you would like them to do for you.

Luke 6:28-31

The Lord is kind and merciful, slow to get angry, full of unfailing love.

Follow God's example in everything you do. . . . Live a life filled with love for others, following the example of Christ, who loved you.

Be kind to each other, tenderhearted, forgiving one another, just as God through Christ has forgiven you.

You can have sincere love for each other as brothers and sisters because you were cleansed from your sins when you accepted the truth of the Good News. So see to it that you really do love each other intensely with all your hearts.

Psalm 145:8; Ephesians 5:1-2; 4:32; 1 Peter 1:22

NOVEMBER 13

NOVEMBER
14

I have loved you even as the Father has loved me. Remain in my love. When you obey me, you remain in my love, just as I obey my Father and remain in his love. I have told you this so that you will be filled with my joy. Yes, your joy will overflow!

I command you to love each other in the same way that I love you. And here is how to measure it—the greatest love is shown when people lay down their lives for their friends.

John 15:9-13

Living is for Christ, and dying is even better.

I'm torn between two desires: Sometimes I want to live, and sometimes I long to go and be with Christ.

We know that as long as we live in these bodies we are not at home with the Lord.

Philippians 1:21, 23; 2 Corinthians 5:6

16

I will thank you, Lord, in front of all the people. I will sing your praises among the nations. **For your unfailing love is higher than the heavens.** Your faithfulness reaches to the clouds. Be exalted, O God, above the highest heavens. May your glory shine over all the earth.

Psalm 108:3-5

17

NOVEMBER

Who in all of heaven can compare with the Lord? What mightiest angel is anything like the Lord?

O Lord God Almighty! **Where is there anyone as mighty as you, Lord?** Faithfulness is your very character.

All heaven will praise your miracles, Lord; myriads of angels will praise you for your faithfulness.

Psalm 89:6, 8, 5

From the time the world was created, people have seen the earth and sky and all that God made. They can clearly see his invisible qualities—his eternal power and divine nature.

Day after day they continue to speak; night after night they make him known. They speak without a sound or a word; their voice is silent in the skies.

When I look at the night sky and see the work of your fingers—the moon and the stars you have set in place—what are mortals that you should think of us, mere humans that you should care for us?

When Adam sinned, sin entered the entire human race. Adam's sin brought death, so death spread to everyone, for everyone sinned.

God so loved the world that he gave his only Son, so that everyone who believes in him will not perish but have eternal life.

Romans 1:20; Psalm 19:2-3; 8:3-4; Romans 5:12; John 3:16

18

19

november

When people work, their wages are not a gift. Workers earn what they receive. **But people are declared righteous because of their faith, not because of their work.**

King David spoke of this, describing the happiness of an undeserving sinner who is declared to be righteous: "Oh, what joy for those whose disobedience is forgiven, whose sins are put out of sight."

Romans 4:4-7

When God promised Abraham that he would become the father of many nations, Abraham believed him.

And Abraham's faith did not weaken, even though he knew that he was too old to be a father at the age of one hundred and that Sarah, his wife, had never been able to have children.

He was absolutely convinced that God was able to do anything he promised. And because of Abraham's faith, God declared him to be righteous.

Romans 4:18-19, 21-22

21

NOVEMBER

We are [God's] offspring. . . . We shouldn't
think of God as an idol designed by craftsmen
from gold or silver or stone.

**God is so rich in mercy, and he loved us
so very much, that even while we were
dead because of our sins, he gave us life
when he raised Christ from the dead.**

For we are God's masterpiece. He has
created us anew in Christ Jesus, so that we
can do the good things he planned for us
long ago.

Acts 17:28-29; Ephesians 2:4-5, 10

Live clean, innocent lives as children of God in a dark world full of crooked and perverse people. **Let your lives shine brightly before them.** Hold tightly to the word of life.

Those who are wise will shine as bright as the sky, and those who turn many to righteousness will shine like stars forever.

Philippians 2:15-16; Daniel 12:3

22
NOVEMBER

23

As God's messenger, I give each of you this warning: Be honest in your estimate of yourselves, measuring your value by how much faith God has given you.

What makes you better than anyone else? What do you have that God hasn't given you? **And if all you have is from God, why boast as though you have accomplished something on your own?**

The proud will be humbled, but the humble will be honored.

So humble yourselves before God. Resist the Devil, and he will flee from you. Draw close to God, and God will draw close to you.

Romans 12:3; 1 Corinthians 4:7; Luke 18:14; James 4:7-8

24
NOVEMBER

For wisdom is far more valuable than rubies. Nothing you desire can be compared with it.

"I, Wisdom, live together with good judgment. I know where to discover knowledge and discernment."

Leave your foolish ways behind, and begin to live; learn how to be wise.

Wisdom will multiply your days and add years to your life.

Proverbs 8:11-12; 9:6, 11

Seek his will in all you do, and he will direct your paths.

Don't be impressed with your own wisdom. Instead, fear the Lord and turn your back on evil. Then you will gain renewed health and vitality.

Proverbs 3:6-8

NOVEMBER
25

NOVEMBER
26

Just as you accepted Christ Jesus as your Lord,
you must continue to live in obedience to him.
**Let your roots grow down into him and draw
up nourishment from him, so you will grow
in faith, strong and vigorous in the truth
you were taught.** Let your lives overflow with
thanksgiving for all he has done.

Colossians 2:6-7

27 NOVEMBER

You must be even more careful to put into action God's saving work in your lives, obeying God with deep reverence and fear. For God is working in you, giving you the desire to obey him and the power to do what pleases him.

Let God transform you into a new person by changing the way you think. Then you will know what God wants you to do, and you will know how good and pleasing and perfect his will really is.

Philippians 2:12-13; Romans 12:2

Take delight in the Lord, and he will give you your heart's desire. **Commit everything you do to the Lord.** Trust him, and he will help you.

Don't be impatient for the Lord to act! Travel steadily along his path. He will honor you, giving you the land.

A wonderful future lies before those who love peace.

Psalm 37:4-5, 34, 37

If you give special attention and a good seat to the rich person, . . . doesn't this discrimination show that you are guided by wrong motives?

Hasn't God chosen the poor in this world to be rich in faith? Aren't they the ones who will inherit the kingdom he promised to those who love him?

Yes indeed, it is good when you truly obey our Lord's royal command found in the Scriptures: "Love your neighbor as yourself." But if you pay special attention to the rich, you are committing a sin, for you are guilty of breaking that law.

James 2:3-5, 8-9

Someone called from the crowd, "Teacher, please tell my brother to divide our father's estate with me."

Jesus replied, "Friend, who made me a judge over you to decide such things as that? . . . Beware! Don't be greedy for what you don't have. **Real life is not measured by how much we own."**

True religion with contentment is great wealth. After all, we didn't bring anything with us when we came into the world, and we certainly cannot carry anything with us when we die. So if we have enough food and clothing, let us be content.

Luke 12:13-15; 1 Timothy 6:6-8

30

december

Morning, noon, and night I plead aloud in my distress, and the Lord hears my voice.

Go away by yourself, shut the door behind you, and pray to your Father secretly. Then your Father, who knows all secrets, will reward you.

Daniel . . . went home and knelt down as usual in his upstairs room. . . . He prayed three times a day, just as he had always done, giving thanks to his God.

The earnest prayer of a righteous person has great power and wonderful results.

Psalm 55:17; Matthew 6:6; Daniel 6:10; James 5:16

DECEMBER

2

Those the Father has given me will come to me, and I will never reject them. For it is my Father's will that all who see his Son and believe in him should have eternal life.

Trust in the Lord with all your heart; do not depend on your own understanding. Seek his will in all you do, and he will direct your paths.

John 6:37, 40; Proverbs 3:5-6

3 DECEMBER

Happy are those who have the God of Israel as their helper, whose hope is in the Lord their God.

The Lord watches over those who fear him, those who rely on his unfailing love. He rescues them from death and keeps them alive in times of famine.

For God has said, "I will never fail you. I will never forsake you." That is why we can say with confidence, "The Lord is my helper."

Psalm 146:5; 33:18-19; Hebrews 13:5-6

The eyes of the Lord watch over those who do right; his ears are open to their cries for help.

The righteous face many troubles, but the Lord rescues them from each and every one.

For the Lord watches over the path of the godly, but the path of the wicked leads to destruction.

Psalm 34:15, 19; 1:6

DECEMBER 4

5

Don't worry about everyday life—whether you have enough food, drink, and clothes. Doesn't life consist of more than food and clothing? Look at the birds. They don't need to plant or harvest or put food in barns because your heavenly Father feeds them. **And you are far more valuable to him than they are.**

And why worry about your clothes? Look at the lilies and how they grow. They don't work or make their clothing. And if God cares so wonderfully for flowers that are here today and gone tomorrow, won't he more surely care for you?

Matthew 6:25-26, 28, 30

6
DECEMBER

The Lord is good. When trouble comes, he is a strong refuge. And he knows everyone who trusts in him.

The angel of God called to Hagar from the sky, "Hagar, what's wrong? Do not be afraid! God has heard the boy's cries from the place where you laid him."

Then God opened Hagar's eyes, and she saw a well. She immediately filled her water container and gave the boy a drink.

The Lord is good to everyone. He showers compassion on all his creation.

Nahum 1:7; Genesis 21:17, 19; Psalm 145:9

When [Peter] looked around at the high waves, he was terrified and began to sink. "Save me, Lord!" he shouted.

Instantly Jesus reached out his hand and grabbed him. "You don't have much faith," Jesus said. "Why did you doubt me?"

The steps of the godly are directed by the Lord. **He delights in every detail of their lives.** Though they stumble, they will not fall, for the Lord holds them by the hand.

Give all your worries and cares to God, for he cares about what happens to you.

Matthew 14:30-31; Psalm 37:23-24; 1 Peter 5:7

DECEMBER

7

DECEMBER
8

We know that God causes everything to work together for the good of those who love God and are called according to his purpose for them. **God will give us our full rights as his children, including the new bodies he has promised us.** He will remove all of their sorrows, and there will be no more death or sorrow or crying or pain.

Romans 8:28, 23; Revelation 21:4

9 DECEMBER

Cling tightly to your faith in Christ, and always keep your conscience clear.

Keep away from anything that might take God's place in your hearts.

Worship no other gods, but only the Lord, for he is a God who is passionate about his relationship with you.

Worship and serve him with your whole heart and with a willing mind. For the Lord sees every heart and understands and knows every plan and thought.

1 Timothy 1:19; 1 John 5:21; Exodus 34:14; 1 Chronicles 28:9

Stay away from idols! I am the one who looks after you and cares for you. I am like a tree that is always green, giving my fruit to you all through the year.

Let those who are wise understand these things. Let those who are discerning listen carefully. **The paths of the Lord are true and right, and righteous people live by walking in them.** But sinners stumble and fall along the way.

Hosea 14:8-9

11
DECEMBER

Remember that those who do good prove that they are God's children.

Don't be impatient for the Lord to act! Travel steadily along his path. He will honor you, giving you the land.

Look at those who are honest and good, for a wonderful future lies before those who love peace.

3 John 1:11; Psalm 37:34, 37

Share each other's troubles and problems, and in this way obey the law of Christ.

Be humble, thinking of others as better than yourself.

Be kind to each other, tenderhearted, forgiving one another, just as God through Christ has forgiven you.

Those who say they live in God should live their lives as Christ did.

Galatians 6:2; Philippians 2:3; Ephesians 4:32; 1 John 2:6

DECEMBER

12

december

13

So you should not be like cowering, fearful slaves. **You should behave instead like God's very own children, adopted into his family—calling him "Father, dear Father."** For his Holy Spirit speaks to us deep in our hearts and tells us that we are God's children.

This expectation will not disappoint us. For we know how dearly God loves us.

Romans 8:15-16; Romans 5:5

14

DECEMBER

The Lord is my shepherd; I have everything I need.
He lets me rest in green meadows; he leads me
beside peaceful streams.

**Give all your worries and cares to God, for
he cares about what happens to you.**

Commit everything you do to the Lord. Trust
him, and he will help you.

Seek his will in all you do, and he will direct
your paths.

Psalm 23:1-2; 1 Peter 5:7; Psalm 37:5;
Proverbs 3:6

15
DECEMBER

Be an example to all believers in what you teach, in the way you live, in your love, your faith, and your purity.

I will teach you wisdom's ways and lead you in straight paths. **If you live a life guided by wisdom, you won't limp or stumble as you run.**

Our lives are in his hands, and he keeps our feet from stumbling.

1 Timothy 4:12; Proverbs 4:11-12; Psalm 66:9

Great is the Lord! He is most worthy
of praise!
The Lord made the heavens!
Honor and majesty surround him;
strength and beauty are in his
dwelling.
O nations of the world, recognize the
Lord,
recognize that the Lord is glorious
and strong.
Tell all the nations that the
Lord is king.

1 Chronicles 16:25-28, 31

16
DECEMBER

17

Yours, O Lord, is the greatness, the power, the glory, the victory, and the majesty. Everything in the heavens and on earth is yours, O Lord, and this is your kingdom.

We adore you as the one who is over all things. Riches and honor come from you alone, for you rule over everything. Power and might are in your hand.

1 Chronicles 29:11-12

18
DECEMBER

[God] alone has all wisdom and power. He determines the course of world events; he removes kings and sets others on the throne. **He gives wisdom to the wise and knowledge to the scholars.**

By his mighty power at work within us, he is able to accomplish infinitely more than we would ever dare to ask or hope.

Daniel 2:20-21; Ephesians 3:20

Some nations boast of their armies and weapons, but we boast in the Lord our God.

From the greatest to the lowliest—all are nothing in his sight. If you weigh them on the scales, they are lighter than a puff of air.

Our lives are in his hands, and he keeps our feet from stumbling.

For he satisfies the thirsty and fills the hungry with good things.

Psalm 20:7; 62:9; 66:9; 107:9

DECEMBER
19

DECEMBER
20

The world and all its people belong to him.

All the animals of the forest are [his], . . . the cattle on a thousand hills. Every bird of the mountains and all the animals of the field.

So don't worry about tomorrow, for tomorrow will bring its own worries. Today's trouble is enough for today.

He will give you all you need from day to day if you live for him and make the Kingdom of God your primary concern.

Psalm 24:1; 50:10-11; Matthew 6:34, 33

21 DECEMBER

Clothe yourselves with tenderhearted mercy.
You will be glorifying God through your
generous gifts. For your generosity to them will
prove that you are obedient to the Good News
of Christ. And they will pray for you with deep
affection because of the wonderful grace of God
shown through you.

Colossians 3:12; 2 Corinthians 9:13-14

God showed how much he loved us by sending his only Son into the world so that we might have eternal life through him. This is real love.

Long ago, even before he made the world, God loved us and chose us in Christ to be holy and without fault in his eyes. His unchanging plan has always been to adopt us into his own family by bringing us to himself through Jesus Christ. And this gave him great pleasure.

1 John 4:9-10; Ephesians 1:4-5

23

DECEMBER

Now this is how Jesus the Messiah was born. His mother, Mary, was engaged to be married to Joseph. But while she was still a virgin, she became pregnant by the Holy Spirit. Joseph, her fiancé, being a just man, decided to break the engagement quietly, so as not to disgrace her publicly.

As he considered this, he fell asleep, and an angel of the Lord appeared to him in a dream. "Joseph, son of David," the angel said, "do not be afraid to go ahead with your marriage to Mary. For the child within her has been conceived by the Holy Spirit. **And she will have a son, and you are to name him Jesus, for he will save his people from their sins.**"

Matthew 1:18-21

[Mary] gave birth to her first child, a son. She wrapped him snugly in strips of cloth and laid him in a manger, because there was no room for them in the village inn.

That night some shepherds were in the fields outside the village, guarding their flocks of sheep. Suddenly, an angel of the Lord appeared among them, and the radiance of the Lord's glory surrounded them. They were terribly frightened, but the angel reassured them.

"Don't be afraid!" he said. **"I bring you good news of great joy for everyone!** The Savior—yes, the Messiah, the Lord—has been born tonight in Bethlehem, the city of David!"

Luke 2:7-11

24

25
december

Thank God for his Son—a gift too wonderful for words!

Shout with joy to the Lord, O earth! Worship the Lord with gladness. Come before him, singing with joy.

Enter his gates with thanksgiving; go into his courts with praise. Give thanks to him and bless his name.

For a child is born to us, a son is given to us. And the government will rest on his shoulders. These will be his royal titles: Wonderful Counselor, Mighty God, Everlasting Father, Prince of Peace.

2 Corinthians 9:15; Psalm 100:1-2, 4; Isaiah 9:6

You are to name him Jesus, for he will save his people from their sins.

He was wounded and crushed for our sins. He was beaten that we might have peace. He was whipped, and we were healed! All of us have strayed away like sheep. We have left God's paths to follow our own. Yet the Lord laid on him the guilt and sins of us all.

He was oppressed and treated harshly, yet he never said a word. . . . From prison and trial they led him away to his death.

He came . . . to remove the power of sin forever by his sacrificial death for us.

In this man Jesus there is forgiveness for your sins.

Matthew 1:21; Isaiah 53:5-8; Hebrews 9:26; Acts 13:38

27

DECEMBER

God in his gracious kindness declares us not guilty. He has done this through Christ Jesus, who has freed us by taking away our sins. For God sent Jesus to take the punishment for our sins and to satisfy God's anger against us. We are made right with God when we believe that Jesus shed his blood, sacrificing his life for us. God was being entirely fair and just when he did not punish those who sinned in former times.

God saved you by his special favor when you believed. And you can't take credit for this; it is a gift from God.

Romans 3:24-25; Ephesians 2:8

Your attitude should be the same that Christ Jesus had. Though he was God, he did not demand and cling to his rights as God. He made himself nothing; he took the humble position of a slave and appeared in human form. And in human form he obediently humbled himself even further by dying a criminal's death on a cross.

Philippians 2:5-8

28

DECEMBER

29

Christ, when he came into the world, said, "'Look, I have come to do your will.'"

Because of this, God raised him up to the heights of heaven and gave him a name that is above every other name, so that **at the name of Jesus every knee will bow, in heaven and on earth and under the earth, and every tongue will confess that Jesus Christ is Lord, to the glory of God the Father.**

Hebrews 10:5, 7; Philippians 2:9-11

30
DECEMBER

Let me say one more thing as I close this letter. **Fix your thoughts on what is true and honorable and right.** Think about things that are pure and lovely and admirable. Think about things that are excellent and worthy of praise.

You must remain faithful to the things you have been taught.

The Lord will stay with you as long as you stay with him! Whenever you seek him, you will find him.

Philippians 4:8; 2 Timothy 3:14; 2 Chronicles 15:2

Christ will be revealed from heaven by the blessed and only almighty God, the King of kings and Lord of lords. He alone can never die.

The Lord is robed in majesty and armed with strength. The world is firmly established.

His power is great.

Your throne, O Lord, has been established from time immemorial. You yourself are from the everlasting past.

Yours . . . is the greatness, the power, the glory, the victory, and the majesty.

1 Timothy 6:15-16; Psalm 93:1; Nahum 1:3; Psalm 93:2; 1 Chronicles 29:11

DECEMBER 31

WheRe AdvEnture beGins with a BoOk!

LoG oN @ Cool2Read.com

Proxine